STUDY GUIDE

Jenifer Kunz

West Texas A&M University

RACIAL AND ETHNIC GROUPS

ELEVENTH EDITION

Richard T. Schaefer

DePaul University

PEARSON

Prentice Hall

Upper Saddle River, New Jersey 07458

© 2008 by PEARSON EDUCATION, INC.
Upper Saddle River, New Jersey 07458

ISBN 0-13-243877-1

Printed in the United States of America

CONTENTS

Chapter One

Understanding Race and Ethnicity

CHAPTER OBJECTIVES
- To become familiar with the factors that determine a dominant and a subordinate group
- To understand the characteristics of minority group members
- To understand the role of power and privilege in relations between a minority and a majority
- To learn about the different types of subordinate groups
- To become familiar with the complexity and the social importance of race
- To evaluate whether or not race really matters in our society
- To understand how race is socially constructed
- To understand the role of stratification and its influence on race and ethnicity
- To be introduced to the different sociological perspectives regarding intergroup relations
- To understand how subordinate groups are created
- To evaluate and understand the consequence of minority group status
- To understand the importance of the processes that create dominant and subordinate groups
- To evaluate the arguments for and against bilingualism and bilingual programs
- To evaluate and understand to process of resistance and change of dominant and subordinate groups

CHAPTER OUTLINE
I.   What Is a Subordinate Group?
- In sociology, *minority* means the same as *subordinate*, and *dominant* is used interchangeably with *majority*.
- Five characteristics of a minority or subordinate group are identified: unequal treatment, distinguishing physical or cultural traits, involuntary membership, awareness of subordination, and in-group marriage.

II.   Types of Subordinate Groups
    A.   Racial Groups
- Two crucial words are identified in the definition of race: *obvious and physical*. However, each society defines what it finds obvious. The designation of a racial group emphasizes physical differences as opposed to cultural distinctions.

B. Ethnic Groups
- Ethnic groups are differentiated from the dominant group on the basis of cultural differences.
C. Listen to Our Voices: The Problem of the Color Line
D. Religious Groups
- Association with a religion other than the dominant faith is another basis for minority group status.
E. Gender Groups
- Males are the social majority; females, although more numerous, are relegated to the position of the social minority. Women encounter prejudice and discrimination and are physically distinguishable.
F. Other Subordinate Groups
- Age, disabilities, and sexual orientation are among factors that are used to subordinate.

III. Does Race Matter?
A. Biological Meaning
- Biologically there are no pure, distinct races. The question of whether races have different innate levels of intelligence has led to explosive controversy. The debate concerning the accuracy of *IQ* tests continues.
B. Social Construction of Race
- Race is important because of the social meaning people have attached to it.

IV. Sociology and the Study of Race and Ethnicity
A. Stratification by Class and Gender
- All societies are characterized by members having unequal amounts of wealth, prestige, and power. Sociologists have observed that entire groups may be assigned to have less or more of what a society values.
B. Theoretical Perspectives
- The *functionalist perspective* emphasizes how parts of society are structured to maintain its stability. Five functions that racial beliefs have for the dominant groups are identified. Six dysfunctions of racism are also identified.
- The *conflict perspective* assumes that the social structure is best understood in terms of conflict or tension between competing groups. According to the conflict perspective, competition takes place between groups with unequal amounts of economic or political power. In the *American Dilemma*, Gunnar Myrdal concluded that the plight of the subordinate group is the responsibility of the dominant majority.
- The *labeling approach* is related to the conflict perspective and is concerned over blaming the victim. *Labeling theory* is an attempt to explain why certain people are viewed as deviant and others engaging in the same behavior are not.

V.   The Creation of Subordinate-Group Status
      A.   Migration
            • Three concepts are differentiated—migration, emigration, and
              immigration.
      B.   Annexation
            • Annexation is common during wars as nations incorporate or attach
              land.
      C.   Colonialism
            • *Colonialism*, or the maintenance of political, social, economic, and
              cultural dominance over people by a foreign power for an extended
              period of time, is the most common way for one group of people to
              dominate another.

VI.   The Consequences of Subordinate-Group Status
      A.   Extermination
            • The most extreme way of dealing with a subordinate group is to
              eliminate it. Examples of *genocide* and *ethnic cleansing* are discussed.
      B.   Expulsion
            • Dominant groups may choose to force a specific subordinate group to
              leave certain areas or even vacate a country.
      C.   Secession
            • A group ceases to be subordinate when it secedes to form a new nation
              or moves to an already established nation, where it becomes dominant.
      D.   Segregation
            • *Segregation* refers to the physical separation of two groups in
              residence, workplace, and social functions. Generally the dominant
              group imposes segregation on a subordinate group. Sociologists
              measure racial segregation using a segregation index or index of
              dissimilarity. White-Black and White-Latino segregation in housing in
              certain metropolitan areas is presented.
      E.   Fusion
            • *Fusion* occurs when a minority and a majority group combine to form
              a new group. This combining can be expressed as A+B+C=D.
              Amalgamation is a form of fusion involving intermarriage. The
              concepts of fusion and amalgamation are often expressed in the term
              melting pot.
      F.   Assimilation
            • *Assimilation* is the process by which a subordinate individual or group
              takes on the characteristics of the dominant group and is eventually
              accepted as part of that group. Assimilation is a majority ideology in
              which A+B+C=A.
      G.   The Pluralist Perspective
            • *Pluralism* implies that various groups in a society have mutual respect
              for one another's culture, a respect that allows minorities to express
              their own culture without suffering prejudice or hostility.

VII. Who Am I?
- The diversity of the United States today has made it more difficult for many people to place themselves on the racial and ethnic landscape. Panethnicity is the development of solidarity between ethnic subgroups. Another challenge to identity is marginality, or the status of being between two cultures.
  A.   Research Focus: Measuring Multiculturalism

VIII. Resistance and Change
- Subordinate groups do not merely accept the definitions and ideology proposed by the dominant group. In the United States there are many examples of resistance and also the promotion of change on the part of subordinate groups.
- This chapter has attempted to organize an approach to subordinate-dominant relations in the United States. The contrasting perspectives of W.E.B. DuBois and Booker T. Washington, offered over a century ago, resonate in our society today.

KEY TERMS

Afrocentric perspective (p. 33)	conflict perspective (p. 17)
amalgamation (p. 25)	dysfunction (p. 17)
assimilation (p. 25)	emigration (p. 20)
bilingualism (p. 28)	ethnic cleansing (p. 29)
biological race (p. 12)	ethnic group (p. 9)
blaming the victim (p. 18)	globalization (p. 20)
class (p. 15)	functionalist perspective (p. 16)
colonialism (p. 21)	fusion (p. 25)
genocide (p. 22)	pluralism (p. 26)
immigration (p. 20)	racial formation (p. 15)
intelligence quotient (p. 22)	racial group (p. 8)
internal colonialism (p. 22)	racism (p. 14)
labeling theory (p. 18)	segregation (p. 23)

4

marginality (p. 31)   self-fulfilling prophecy (p. 19)

melting pot (p. 25)   sociology (p. 15)

migration (p. 20)   stereotypes (p. 18)

minority group (p. 7)   stratification (p. 15)

panethnicity (p. 30)   world systems theory (p. 21)

PRACTICE TESTS

Practice Test One

True-False

1.   T F   In 2000, Hispanics (or Latinos) represented a larger racial/ethnic group than Blacks (or African Americans).
2.   T F   Biologically there are no pure, distinct races.
3.   T F   In the book *American Dilemma*, Gunnar Myrdal concluded that the plight of the subordinate group is the responsibility of the dominant group.
4.   T F   The melting pot refers to the process by which a subordinate individual or group takes on the characteristics of the dominant group and is eventually accepted by the members of that group.
5.   T F   In the 2000 Census, over ten percent of the United States' population selected two or more racial categories.

Multiple Choice

1.   Minority groups are subordinated in terms of _____.
   A. power and privilege
   B. hatred and prejudice
   C. means and ends
   D. discrimination and assimilation

2.   The hierarchical system for possession of wealth, prestige, or power is called:
   A. ethnic groups
   B. stratification
   C. age
   D. functionalism

3.   The two crucial words in the definition of a racial group are
      A. unequal and discriminate.
      B. obvious and physical.
      C. cultural and practice.
      D. heritage and hierarchy.

4.   Groups set apart from others because of their national origin or distinctive
      cultural patterns are known as
      A. ethnic groups.
      B. racial groups.
      C. minority groups.
      D. subordinate groups.

5.   A 1994 book containing a discussion on links between race and IQ was made
      even more controversial by including suggestions that involved ending welfare
      to discourage births among low-IQ poor women and changing immigration
      laws. This book was entitled
      A. *Supreme Thinking*.
      B. *Rethinking America*.
      C. *The Race to Success*.
      D. *The Bell Curve*.

6.   The _____ perspective emphasizes how the parts of society are structured
      to maintain its stability.
      A. interactionist
      B. conflict
      C. functionalist
      D. labeling

7.   _____ theory is an attempt to explain why certain people are viewed as
      deviant and others engaging in the same behavior are not.
      A. Exchange
      B. Labeling
      C. Conflict
      D. Functionalist

8.   _____ refers to the maintenance of political, social, economic, and cultural
      dominance over people by a foreign power.
      A. Colonialism
      B. Annexation
      C. Immigration
      D. Emigration

9. On the Intergroup Relations Continuum, extermination is on one end and _____ is on the other end.
   A. segregation
   B. assimilation
   C. pluralism
   D. secession

10. _____ refers to the status of being between two cultures.
    A. Ethnocentrism
    B. Cultural relativism
    C. Panethnicity
    D. Marginality

Short-Answer Questions
1. What is a subordinate group? Identify the basic characteristics of a subordinate group.
2. What are the types of subordinate groups identified in the text? Are there any additional subordinate groups you would add? Are there any listed you would delete? Explain your selections.
3. According to the author of the text, if race does not distinguish humans from one another biologically, why does it seem to be so important? How would you answer this question?
4. Write a paragraph in which you try to explain the data presented in *Figure 1.6*.
5. According to the *functionalists*, what are two functions that racial beliefs have for the dominant group?

Practice Test Two

True-False
1. T F According to the author, the relations between racial and ethnic groups are much like relations between family members.
2. T F According to the author, race is a socially constructed group.
3. T F Emigration describes leaving a country to live in another.
4. T F The top five of the "Most White-Black Segregated Metropolitan Areas in the United States" are found in the South.
5. T F Panethnicity is the development of solidarity between ethnic subgroups.

Multiple Choice
1. The largest percentage of Asian Americans are
   A. Japanese.
   B. Korean.
   C. Chinese.
   D. Filipino.

2. In sociology, minority means the same as subordinate, and _____ is used interchangeably with majority.
    A. superior
    B. elite
    C. dominant
    D. manifest

3. According to W.E.B. DuBois, the problem of the twentieth century was to become the problem of
    A. religion.
    B. hate.
    C. the color line.
    D. gender inequality.

4. The _____ perspective suggests competition takes place between groups with unequal amounts of economic and political power.
    A. functional
    B. conflict
    C. interactionist
    D. exchange

5. _____ are unreliable generalizations about all members of a group that do not take individual differences into account.
    A. Stereotypes
    B. Stigmas
    C. Labels
    D. Correlations

6. Nations, particularly during wars or as a result of war, incorporate or attach land. This is known as
    A. annexation.
    B. colonialism.
    C. world system theory.
    D. fusion.

7. _____ theory views the global economic system as divided between nations that control wealth and those that provide natural resources and labor.
    A. Developmental
    B. World Systems
    C. Functional
    D. Structural

8.   Theoretically, _____ does not entail intermarriage, but it is very similar to amalgamation.
    A. fusion
    B. assimilation
    C. segregation
    D. pluralism

9.   Assimilation does not occur at the same pace for all groups. Assimilation tends to take longer with all of the following conditions except when:
    A. the differences between the minority and majority are large.
    B. the minority arrives in a short period of time.
    C. the arrival is recent, and the homeland is accessible.
    D. the minority-group residents are dispersed rather than concentrated.

10.   The most common multiple identity in terms of "race choices" in the 2000 census was
    A. White and Black.
    B. White and American Indian and Alaskan Native Americans.
    C. Black and Hispanic.
    D. Asian and White.

Short-Answer Questions
1.   What are three problems with the validity of IQ tests?
2.   Identify, define, and illustrate three consequences of subordinate group status.
3.   What are three factors that tend to make assimilation take longer than it otherwise would?
4.   Write a paragraph discussing the problems with measuring multiculturalism found in the "Research Focus Box" on pages 30-31.
5.   Identify two commonly-held stereotypes for a particular subordinate group and find empirical evidence that contradicts these stereotypes.

ANSWERS TO PRACTICE TEST QUESTIONS

Practice Test One

True-False		**Multiple Choice**			
1	T (p. 5)	1.	A (p. 7)	6.	C (p. 16)
2	T (p. 13)	2.	B (p. 15)	7.	B (p. 18)
3	T (p. 18)	3.	B (p. 8)	8.	A (p. 21)
4	F (p. 25)	4.	A (p. 9)	9.	C (p. 22)
5	F (p. 30)	5.	D (p. 13)	10.	D (p. 31)

Practice Test Two

True-False		**Multiple Choice**			
1	F (p. 5)	1.	C (p. 6)	6.	A (p. 20)
2	T (p. 14)	2.	C (p. 6)	7.	B (p. 21)
3	T (p. 20)	3.	C (p. 10)	8.	A (p. 25)
4	F (p. 24)	4.	B (p. 16)	9.	D (p. 25)
5	T (p. 30)	5.	A (p. 18)	10.	B (p. 26-27)

APPLICATIONS/EXERCISES/ACTIVITIES

1. Distinguish between genocide, expulsion, secession, segregation, fusion, assimilation, and the pluralist perspective and illustrate these concepts by utilizing information that you gather by visiting the following web pages: the Anti-Defamation League at http://www.adl.org, and the American-Arab Anti-Discrimination Committee at http://www.adc.org.

2. Race, ethnicity, sex, and religion are not the only basis for prejudice and discrimination. Groups like political radicals, ex-mental patients, and alcoholics are subject to stereotyping. See the application of the social distance scale to such groups in J. L. Simmon's Deviants. Berkeley: Glendessary Press, 1969: 28-35.

Chapter 1 – Understanding Race and Ethnicity

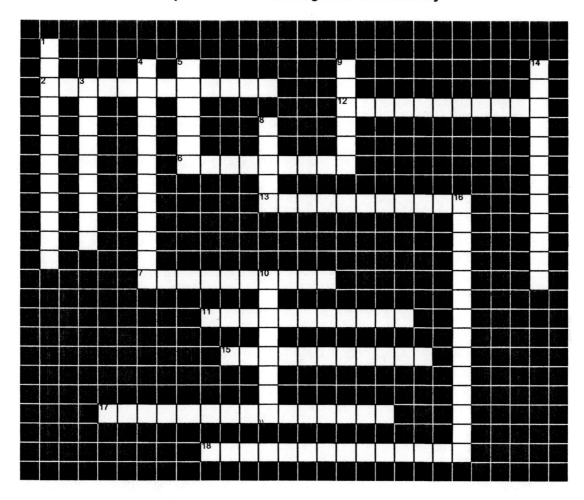

Across:

2 The process by which a subordinate individual or group takes on the characteristics of the dominant group

6 A general term that describes any transfer of population

7 Diverse racial or ethnic groups or both, forming a new creation, a new cultural entity

11 A group set apart from others because of its national origin or distinctive cultural patterns

12 The physical separation of two groups, often imposed on a subordinate group by the dominant group

13 Unreliable, exaggerated generalizations about all members of a group that do not take individual differences into account

15 A group that is socially set apart because of obvious physical differences

17 Policy of ethnic Serbs to eliminate Muslims from parts of Bosnia

18 A theory to explain why certain people are viewed as deviants and others engaging in the same behavior are not

Down:

1 The process by which a dominant group and a subordinate group combine through intermarriage to form a new group

3 The systematic study of social behavior and human groups

4 The use of two or more languages in places of work or education and the treatment of each language as legitimate

5 A doctrine that one race is superior

8 As defined by Max Weber, people who share similar levels of wealth

9 A minority and a majority group combining to form a new group

10 The deliberate systematic killing of an entire people or nation

14 The development of solidarity between ethnic subgroups, as reflected in the terms Hispanic or Asian American

16 A structured ranking of entire groups of people that perpetuates unequal rewards and power in a society

Chapter Two

Prejudice

CHAPTER OBJECTIVES
- To understand and become familiar with the concept of hate crimes
- To understand how prejudice plays a role in perceptions of people seen as racially "different"
- To become familiar with the similarities and differences between prejudice and discrimination
- To explore various theories and explanations of prejudice, including exploitation theory, scapegoat theory, authoritarian personality theory, and normative theory
- To identify some possibilities that lead to a reduction of prejudice between groups
- To understand on how potential employers respond to ethnic-sounding names
- To understand and evaluate the concept of racial profiling and the role it may play in prejudice and discrimination
- To evaluate the explore the extent of prejudice in our society
- To evaluate and understand the overall mood of the oppressed
- To understand research findings dealing with intergroup hostility
- To become familiar with possible ways to reduce prejudice in our society
- To identify and understand the ten ways to fight hate

CHAPTER OUTLINE
I. Hate Crimes
- A *hate crime* is defined by the government as a criminal offense committed against a person, property, or society which is motivated, in whole or in part, by the offender's bias against a race, religion, ethnic/national origin group, or sexual orientation group. Recent legislation has added physical and mental disabilities as factors that could be the basis of hate crimes.

II. Prejudice and Discrimination
- *Prejudice* is a negative attitude toward an entire category of people. *Discrimination* involves behavior that excludes all members of a group from certain rights, opportunities, or privileges.
  - A. Merton's Theory
    - Robert Merton developed a typology that points out that attitudes should not be confused with behavior. He identified four different categories illustrating the relationship between attitudes and behavior: all-weather liberal, reluctant liberal, timid bigot, and all-weather bigot.

B.   LaPiere's Study
- This research exposed the relationship between racial attitudes and social conduct. From 1930 to 1932 LaPiere traveled throughout the United States with a Chinese couple, and despite the alleged climate of intolerance of Asians, LaPiere observed the couple being treated politely at hotels, motels, and restaurants.

III.   Theories of Prejudice
A.   Scapegoating Theory
- *Scapegoating theory* says that prejudiced people believe they are society's victims.
B.   Authoritarian Personality Theory
- The *authoritarian personality theory* attempts to detail the prejudiced personality. According to Adorno, the basic characteristics of the authoritarian personality are adherence to conventional values, uncritical acceptance of authority, and concern with power and toughness.
C.   Exploitation Theory
- *Exploitation theory* is part of the Marxist tradition in sociology. According to this view, racial prejudice is often used to justify keeping a group in a subordinate position, such as a lower social class.
D.   Normative Approach
- The *normative approach* takes the view that prejudice is influenced by norms and situations that encourage or discourage the tolerance of minorities.

IV.   The Content of Prejudice: Stereotypes
A.   What are Stereotypes?
- *Stereotypes* are unreliable generalizations about all members of a p that do not take individual differences into account.
B.   Listen to Our Voices: National Media Should Stop Using Obscene Words
C.   Trends in Stereotypes
- The mass media, particularly television, portray stereotypes along racial and ethnic lines in numerous ways. The labeling of individuals has strong implications for the self-fulfilling prophecy. Stereotypes are held by both members of the dominant and subordinate groups.
D.   Stereotyping in Action: Racial Profiling
- According to the Department of Justice, *racial profiling* is any police-initiated action based on race, ethnicity, or national origin rather than the person's behavior. Racial profiling persists despite overwhelming evidence that it is misleading. Talk of legislating against it has however met with firm resistance.

V.   The Extent of Prejudice
      A.   The Social Distance Scale
            • *Social distance* has been defined as the tendency to approach or
              withdraw from a racial group. Emory Bogardus has developed an
              empirical measure of social distance, often referred to as the *Bogardus
              scale*. The scale asks people how willing they would be to interact
              with various racial and ethnic groups in seven specified social
              situations. Each situation describes a different degree of social contact
              or social distance.
      B.   Trends in Prejudice
            • Is prejudice decreasing? The evidence is mixed, with some indicators
              of willingness to give up some old prejudices while new negative
              attitudes emerge. Attitudes are important as a change in attitude may
              create a context in which legislative and behavioral change can occur.

VI.   The Mood of the Oppressed
      • Over the years researchers have seemed to be more interested in White
        attitudes on racial issues than they have been on the attitudes of subordinate
        group members. Recent research has offered insight into sharply different
        attitudes between the dominant and subordinate groups. Assessment on self-
        esteem of minorities has been misleading.

VII. Intergroup Hostility
      • A national survey revealed that, like Whites, many African Americans,
        Hispanic Americans, and Asian Americans held prejudiced and stereotypical
        views of other racial and ethnic minority groups. At the same time, the survey
        also revealed positive views of the major racial and ethnic minorities.
        Curiously, we find that some groups feel they get along better with Whites
        than with other minority groups.

VIII. Reducing Prejudice
      • Focusing on how to eliminate prejudice involves an explicit value judgment:
        prejudice is wrong and causes problems for those who are prejudiced and for
        the victims. For most encouraging research findings as to how to change
        negative attitudes towards groups of people point to the mass media,
        education, intergroup contact, and workplace training programs.
      A.   Education and Mass Media
            • Most research studies show that well-constructed programs do have
              some positive effect in reducing prejudice, at least temporarily. Studies
              have also consistently shown that increased formal education,
              regardless of content, is associated with racial tolerance.
      B.   Equal-Status Contact
            • An impressive number of studies have confirmed the *contact
              hypothesis*, which states that the intergroup contact between people of
              equal status in harmonious circumstances will cause them to become
              less prejudiced and to abandon previously held stereotypes. A key

factor in reducing hostility in addition to equal-status contact is the presence of a common goal.

C. Corporate Response: Diversity Training
- Workplace hostility can lead to lost productivity and even attrition. It can also lead to the development of a reputation of having a "chilly climate" which discourages both qualified people of color or women from applying for jobs and potential clients seeking products or services. In an effort to improve workplace relations, most organizations have initiated some form of diversity training. The effectiveness and the content of diversity programs vary tremendously.

IX. Ways to Fight Hate
- Ways to fight hate include the following: act, unite, support the victims, do your homework, create an alternative, speak up, lobby leaders, look long range, teach tolerance, and dig deeper.
A. Research Focus: What's In a Name?
B. Conclusion
- Prejudice and discrimination are not the same. Several theories try to explain why prejudice exists. Equal-status may reduce hostility between groups. Reducing prejudice is important because it can lead to support for policy change.

KEY TERMS

authoritarian personality (p.45)   hate crime (p. 39)

Bogardus scale (p.51)   normative approach (p.46)

contact hypothesis (p.59)   prejudice (p.41)

discrimination (p.41)   racial profiling (p.50)

ethnocentrism (p.39)   scapegoating theory (p.43)

ethnophaulisms (p.41)   social distance (p.51)

exploitation theory (p.45)   stereotype (p.47)

PRACTICE TESTS

Practice Test One

True-False
1.   T F   *Ethnocentrism* refers to the tendency to assume that one's culture and way of life is superior to all others.
2.   T F   Most *hate crimes* are the result of people acting alone or with a few others.
3.   T F   The *normative approach* takes the view that prejudice is the result of economic competition between unequal groups.
4.   T F   A score of zero on the *social distance scale* indicates no social distance and therefore no prejudice.
5.   T F   The mass media, like schools, may reduce prejudice without the need for specially designed programs.

Multiple Choice
1. _____ is the tendency to assume that one's culture and way of life are superior to all others.
   A. Ethnocentrism
   B. Cultural relativism
   C. Ethnophaulism
   D. Authoritarianism

2. Another term for *ethnic slurs* is
   A. ethnosemantics.
   B. sociolinguistics.
   C. scapegoating.
   D. ethnophaulisms.

3. La Piere's study on the relationship between peoples' beliefs and behavior involved
   A. workplace settings.
   B. traveling the country with an Asian couple.
   C. commuting to work with an African American.
   D. driving across the country on a motorcycle.

4. Which of the following is *not* a characteristic of the *authoritarian personality*?
   A. adherence to conventional values
   B. uncritical acceptance of authority
   C. critical thinking
   D. concern with power and toughness

5.   The _____ theory emphasizes that much prejudice is economically motivated.
     A. normative
     B. authoritarian personality
     C. scapegoat
     D. exploitation

6.   The view that peer and social influences encourage tolerance or intolerance reflects the perspective offered by the _____ theory of prejudice.
     A. normative
     B. scapegoat
     C. authoritarian personality
     D. exploitation

7.   In the "Listen to Our Voices" box, which of the following is Helen Zia discussing?
     A. discrimination
     B. stereotyping
     C. ethnocentrism
     D. racial profiling

8.   Which of the following groups were in the top third of the hierarchy of the *social distance scale* over the last several decades?
     A. White Americans
     B. Indians (from India)
     C. Blacks
     D. Chinese

9.   All of the following are ways to fight hate presented in the chapter except:
     A. dig deeper.
     B. look long range.
     C. support the offender.
     D. unite.

10. The _____ hypothesis states that intergroup contact between people of equal status in harmonious circumstances will cause them to become less prejudiced and to abandon previously held stereotypes.
     A. equality
     B. harmony
     C. contact
     D. circumstantial

Short-Answer Questions

1. How does the government define a *hate crime*?
2. In a paragraph summarize the different theories of prejudice.
3. In what ways do you think television affects prejudice in our society?
4. Describe the basic principles of the *contact hypothesis*?
5. What conclusions are being drawn by the author concerning research on *intergroup hostility* between subordinate groups?

Practice Test Two

True-False

1. T F Race is the apparent motivation in over one-half of all *hate crimes* identified by the police.
2. T F *Prejudice* and *discrimination* are related concepts but are not the same.
3. T F According to Gordon Allport, the *exploitation theory* correctly points the finger at one of the factors in prejudice, that is, the rationalized self-interest of the privileged.
4. T F Studies consistently document that increased formal education, regardless of content, is associated with racial tolerance.
5. T F The Bureau of the Census projects that less than sixty percent of the United States workforce will be White in the year 2008.

Multiple Choice

1. All of the following are explanations of why people become prejudiced except:
   A. social distance theory.
   B. exploitation theory.
   C. authoritarian theory.
   D. normative theory.

2. Which one of the following is not one of the categories found in Robert Merton's typology of prejudice and discrimination?
   A. all-weather liberal
   B. conservative liberal
   C. timid bigot
   D. reluctant liberal

3. _____ theory is criticized for offering little explanation of why a specific group is selected or why frustration is not taken out on the real culprit when possible.
   A. Scapegoat
   B. Normative
   C. Authoritarian personality
   D. Exploitation

4.   A person from an intolerant household is more like to be openly prejudiced—is an example for the _____ theory of prejudice.
     A. exploitation
     B. normative
     C. scapegoating
     D. authoritarian personality

5.   The *Bogardus scale* is a measure of
     A. individual discrimination.
     B. social distance.
     C. institutional discrimination.
     D. racism.

6.   All of the following are methods of reducing prejudice discussed in the text except:
     A. equal status contact.
     B. diversity training.
     C. the contact hypothesis.
     D. resocialization.

7.   Reluctant liberals are those who:
     A. discriminate in an overt fashion.
     B. discriminate if it is socially sanctioned.
     C. harbor prejudice but do not express it.
     D. can express prejudice only in a group.

8.   In 1999, the _____ reported that every new prime time series-26 of them-set to debut in the coming season, would have all the leading characters and most of the supporting casts be white.
     A. *Los Angeles Times*
     B. *New York Times*
     C. *USA Today*
     D. *Washington Post*

9.   According to the book, a _____ is a reputation of a business being unfriendly to people of color or to women and it discourages both qualified people from applying for jobs and potential clients from seeking products or services.
     A. classist climate
     B. sexist climate
     C. racist climate
     D. chilly climate

10. The Bureau of Labor Statistics claims that the largest percentage of foreign-born workers in the United States come
   A. The Philippines
   B. Mexico
   C. India
   D. Canada

Short-Answer Questions

1. According to Robert Merton, what are the four major categories created when studying the relationship between prejudice and discrimination? Provide one illustration for each of these categories.
2. Summarize the research done by LaPiere that supports the typology of prejudice and discrimination created by Robert Merton.
3. Summarize the major points being made by the author concerning *racial profiling*.
4. Briefly describe the *social distance scale*. What are the patterns found in social distance as reported in *Figure 2.4*?
5. According to the author, what roles can the *mass media* and *education* play in our society in *reducing prejudice*?

ANSWERS TO PRACTICE TEST QUESTIONS

Practice Test One

True-False

1. T (p. 19)
2. T (p. 39)
3. F (p. 46)
4. F (p. 51)
5. T (p. 58)

Multiple Choice

1.	A (p. 39)	6.	A (p. 46)
2.	D (p. 41)	7.	B (p. 47)
3.	B (p. 43)	8.	B (p. 51)
4.	C (p. 45)	9.	C (p. 63)
5.	D (p. 45)	10.	C (p. 59)

Practice Test Two

True-False

1. F (p. 39)
2. T (p. 41)
3. T (p. 45)
4. T (p. 58)
5. F (p. 61)

Multiple Choice

1.	A (p. 43)	6.	D (p. 54)
2.	B (p. 42)	7.	C (p. 42)
3.	A (p. 45)	8.	A (p. 58)
4.	B (p. 46)	9.	D (p. 60)
5.	B. (p. 51)	10.	B (p. 61)

APPLICATIONS/EXERCISES/ACTIVITIES

1. How have attitudes of Blacks and whites changed over the years? A U.S. Senator recently made comments that were interpreted as racist and offensive. Visit this site http://people-press.org/reports/display.php3?ReportID=89 Have public statements by elected officials become more subject to scrutiny?

2. Out Groups: The grade school experiment of dividing the classroom into the "privileged blue eyes" and the "subordinate brown eyes" is legendary. Read about this experiment in Allen and Wilder's "Categorization, Belief Similarity, and Intergroup Discrimination" in the *Journal of Personality and Social Psychology*, 32: 971-977

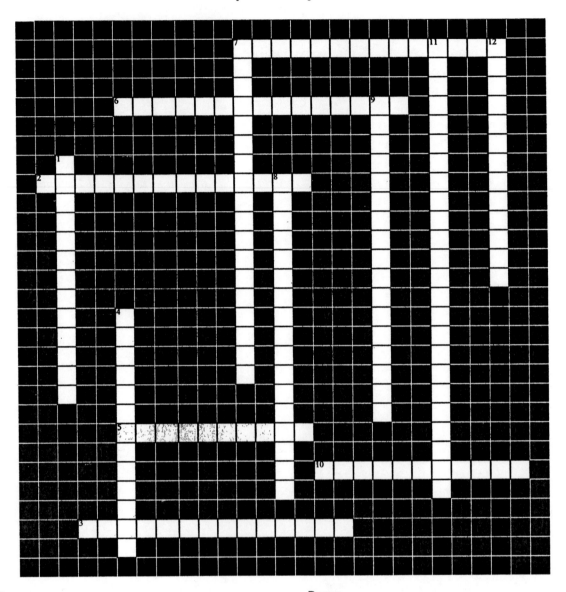

Across:

2 Tendency to approach or withdraw from a racial group

3 The denial of opportunities and equal rights to individuals and groups because of prejudice or for other arbitrary reasons

5 Criminal offense committed because of the offender's bias against a race, religion, ethnic/national origin group, or sexual orientation group

6 Any arbitrary police-initiated action based on race, ethnicity, or natural origin rather than a person's behavior

7 The tendency to approach or withdraw from a racial group

10 Unreliable, exaggerated generalizations about all members of a group that do not take individual differences into account

Down:

1 Technique to measure social distance toward different racial and ethnic groups

2 Early psychological approach that emphasized analysis of immediate experience into basic elements

4 Racial or ethnic slurs, including derisive nicknames

7 A person or group blamed irrationally for another person's or group's problems or difficulties

8 An interactionist perspective stating that intergroup contact between people of equal status in noncompetitive circumstances will reduce prejudice

9 Prejudice is influenced by social norms and situations that encourage or discourage the tolerance of minorities

11 A personality type likely to be prejudiced and to use others as scapegoats

12 The tendency to assume that one's culture and way of life are superior to all others

Chapter Three

Discrimination

CHAPTER OBJECTIVES
- To understand the concepts of discrimination, and relative and absolute deprivation
- To understand some of the explanations of why discrimination occurs
- To become familiar with and to evaluate the different types of discrimination
- To become familiar with the institutional factors that influence inequality
- To understand the consequences of low-wage labor, including, how a large portion of racial and ethnic minorities are among the working poor
- To learn about the factors that can exacerbate one's subordinate status
- To understand the origins and purposes of affirmative action programs
- To understand and evaluate ways to measure discrimination
- To understand and evaluate how wealth inequality is discrimination's legacy
- To become familiar with the ways in which members of subordinate groups respond to situations of institutional discrimination
- To become familiar with the concept of environment justice and its relationship with discrimination
- To evaluate whether or not affirmative action is reverse discrimination
- To become familiar with the concepts of the glass ceiling

CHAPTER OUTLINE
I. Understanding Discrimination
- *Discrimination* is the denial of opportunities and equal rights to individuals and groups because of prejudice or for other arbitrary reasons.
    A. Relative versus Absolute Deprivation
- Conflict theorists have said correctly that it is not absolute, unchanging standards that determine deprivation and oppression. *Relative deprivation* is defined as the conscious experience of a negative discrepancy between legitimate expectations and present actualities. *Absolute deprivation* implies a fixed standard based on a minimum level of subsistence below which families should not be expected to exist.
    B. Total Discrimination
- *Total discrimination* refers to current discrimination operating in the labor market and past discrimination.
    C. Institutional Discrimination
- *Institutional discrimination* is the denial of opportunities and equal rights to individuals and groups that result from the normal operation of a society. Such discrimination is seen as unconscious and widespread.
    D. Listen to Our Voices: Of Race and Risk

II.   Low-Wage Labor
- The *informal economy* consists of transfers of money, goods, and services that are not reported to the government. The informal economy is sometimes called the *irregular* or *underground economy*. According to the *dual labor market* model, minorities have been relegated to the informal economy, with low-paying and low or no-benefit jobs. The workers in the informal economy are ill prepared to enter the primary labor market. A self-fulfilling cycle continues that allows past discrimination to create a separate work environment.

    A.   Research Focus: Discrimination in Job Seeking

III.   Discrimination Today

    A.   Measuring Discrimination
- Income data show vividly the disparity between African Americans and Whites, men and women. *Double jeopardy* refers to the combination of two subordinate statuses, defined as experienced by women of color. Income differences are not simply the result of discrimination in employment. Even when education is held constant, income differences between Blacks and Whites, and between men and women exist. Schooling quality must also be taken into account.

    B.   Eliminating Discrimination
- Two main agents of social change work to reduce discrimination: voluntary associations and the federal government. Most efforts initiated by the government have are urged by associations or organizations representing minority groups.

IV.   Environmental Justice
- *Environmental justice* refers to the efforts to ensure that hazardous substances are controlled so that all communities receive protection regardless of race or socioeconomic circumstance.

V.   Affirmative Action
- *Affirmative action* is the positive effort to recruit subordinate-group members, including women, for jobs, promotions, and educational opportunities.

    A.   Affirmative Action Explained
- Affirmative action has been aimed at institutional discrimination in a number of areas, including restrictive employment leave policies, seniority rules, and nepotism-based membership policies.

    B.   The Legal Debate
- There have been many bitterly contested cases in the courts focusing on the issue of reverse discrimination. Some of the most significant ones are summarized in the table provided in this section of the chapter.

VI.   Reverse Discrimination
- *Reverse discrimination* refers to government actions that cause better-qualified White men to be bypassed in favor of women and minority men. California's Proposition 209, a referendum to amend the state constitution and

prohibit any programs that give preferential treatment to women for minorities for college admission, employment, promotion, or government contracts (passed in 1996), is discussed.

VII.   The Glass Ceiling
- The *glass ceiling* refers to the barrier that blocks the promotion of a qualified worker because of gender or minority membership. Besides glass ceilings there are also *glass walls*, keeping workers from moving laterally. The *glass escalator* refers to the male advantage experienced in occupations dominated by women.
- Discrimination takes its toll. Discrimination takes several forms. Support for eliminating discrimination against minorities seems to be failing.

KEY TERMS

absolute deprivation (p. 69)	informal economy (p. 75)
affirmative action (p. 85)	institutional discrimination (p. 72)
discrimination (p. 69)	irregular or underground economy (p. 75)
income (p. 75)	redlining (p. 82)
dual labor market (p. 75)	relative deprivation (p. 88)
environmental justice (p. 84)	reverse discrimination (p. 68)
glass ceiling (p. 90)	states' rights (p. 81) glass escalator (p. 92)
total discrimination (p. 70)	glass wall (p. 91) wealth (p.83)

PRACTICE TESTS

Practice Test One

True-False
1.   T F   *Absolute deprivation* implies a fixed standard based on a minimum of subsistence below which families should not be expected to exist.
2.   T F   The *informal economy* is also referred to as the dual labor market.
3.   T F   Patricia Williams describes her experience to secure a mortgage despite initial approval after the bank realized she was Black.
4.   T F   The most important legislative effort to eradicate discrimination was the Civil Rights Act of 1964.
5.   T F   National surveys have shown that most people in the United States think that affirmative action has been bad for our society.

Multiple Choice

1. Harvard-educated lawyer Lawrence Otis Graham sought a position as a _____ in exclusive clubs to learn more about contemporary discrimination.
   A. maintenance worker
   B. groundskeeper
   C. waiter
   D. lifeguard

2. The conscience experience of a negative discrepancy between legitimate expectations and experience refers to
   A. relative deprivation.
   B. institutional discrimination.
   C. total discrimination.
   D. absolute discrimination.

3. _____ refers to current discrimination operating in the labor market and past discrimination.
   A. Institutional discrimination
   B. Total discrimination
   C. Absolute discrimination
   D. Relative discrimination

4. IQ tests favoring middle-class students and hiring practices requiring several year's experience at jobs are examples of
   A. relative deprivation.
   B. irregular discrimination.
   C. total discrimination.
   D. institutional discrimination.

5. The median income for White families in 2006 was $64,663. For African American families the corresponding figure was
   A. $33,075.
   B. $39,057.
   C. $37,005.
   D. $43,317.

6. The typical Asian American household earns an estimated ____ compared to $141,000 in a White household.
   A. $119,074.
   B. $159,000.
   C. $126,098.
   D. $134,902.

7.   The first anti-discrimination action at the executive level was
     A. President Johnson's 1966 equal employment program.
     B. President Roosevelt's 1904 wilderness fund.
     C. President Roosevelt's 1943 creation of the Fair Employment Practices Commission.
     D. The 1964 Civil Rights Act.

8.   _____ is a pattern of discrimination against people trying to buy homes in minority and racially changing neighborhoods.
     A. Double jeopardy
     B. Total discrimination
     C. The irregular economy
     D. Redlining

9.   The *Bakke* case (a 1978 United States Supreme Court decision) dealt with the issue of
     A. the glass wall.
     B. the glass ceiling.
     C. redlining.
     D. reverse discrimination.

10. California's Proposition 209, passed in 1996
     A. required quotas in certain pubic job categories.
     B. eliminated the glass ceiling in public jobs for women.
     C. prohibited any programs that gave preferences to women and minorities for college admissions, employment, promotion, or government contracts.
     D. None of the above.

Short-Answer Questions
1.   Briefly discuss the history of anti-discrimination action and legislation in the United States.
2.   Explain how the case of Cynthia Wiggins is an example of discrimination in our society today. How can society address the problem being illustrated in this case?
3.   Explain Patricia J. Williams' view concerning the causes of total discrimination in our society.
4.   Summarize the arguments for and against affirmative action.
5.   Identify and describe an example of anti-discrimination actions taken by each of branches of the government—the executive, the judicial, and the legislative.

Practice Test Two

True-False

1.   T F   Currently thirteen percent of the nation's Black male population is from precluded from voting because of having a convicted felony   status.

2.   T F   The *Brown v. Board of Education* United States Supreme Court case dealt with the issue of reverse discrimination.

3.   T F   Only Hawaii and Wisconsin had enacted laws against sex discrimination before 1964.

4.   T F   Issues of environmental justice are not limited to metropolitan areas.

5.   T F   In 1991 concern about woman and minorities climbing a broken ladder led to the formation of the Glass Ceiling Commission, chaired by the United States Secretary of Labor.

Multiple Choice

1.   The denial of opportunities and equal rights to individuals and groups because of prejudice or for other arbitrary reasons refers to
    A. relative deprivation.
    B. absolute deprivation.
    C. discrimination.
    D. the glass ceiling.

2.   The pattern of discrimination of people trying to buy houses in minority and racially changing neighborhoods is called:
    A. the regular economy.
    B. redlining.
    C. the underground economy.
    D. the primary economy.

3.   The informal economy is sometimes called the
    A. dual labor market.
    B. irregular economy.
    C. underclass
    D. residual economy

4.   Salaries and wages refers to
    A. stocks
    B. prestige
    C. wealth
    D. income

5. All a person's material assets, including land, stocks, and other types of property is called
   A. wealth
   B. prestige
   C. real estate
   D. power

6. The 1954 United States Supreme Court case in _____ stated that separate but equal facilities, including education, were unconstitutional.
   A. *Brown v. Board of Education*
   B. *Dred Scott*
   C. *Martin v. Wilkes*
   D. *Regents of the State of California v. Bakke*

7. The *Civil Rights Act of 1964* concerned discrimination based on
   A. race.
   B. race and sex.
   C. race, creed, and color.
   D. race, color, creed, national origin, and sex.

8. *Environmental justice* focuses on
   A. quality of life issues relating to schools, family, and churches.
   B. hazardous substances.
   C. drugs.
   D. street crime.

9. *Affirmative action* as a phrase was first used in an executive order by which United States President?
   A. George Washington
   B. Ulysses S. Grant
   C. John F. Kennedy
   D. Ronald Reagan

10. Affirmative action had been aimed at *institutional discrimination* in such areas as
    A. height and weight requirements.
    B. seniority rules.
    C. restrictive employment leave policies.
    D. All of the above.

Short-Answer Questions

1.   Identify and describe three examples of *institutional discrimination*.
2.   Describe the connection between the *irregular* or *underground economy* and the dual labor market.
3.   Provide three ways in which *affirmative action* has been aimed at institutional discrimination.
4.   What is *reverse discrimination*? How can society take into account past discrimination while at the same time not penalizing White males in terms of educational and employment opportunities?
5.   Identify three of the barriers involved in the *glass ceiling*. Discuss the relationship between the glass ceiling and the *glass wall*.

ANSWERS TO PRACTICE TEST QUESTIONS

Practice Test One

True-False			Multiple Choice			
1.	T (p. 69)		1.	C (p. 68)	6.	A (p. 80)
2.	F (p. 75)		2.	A (p. 69)	7.	C (p. 81)
3.	F (p. 71)		3.	B (p. 72)	8.	D (p. 82)
4.	T (p. 81)		4.	D (p. 73)	9.	D (p. 87)
5.	F (p. 89)		5.	C (p. 79)	10.	C (p. 89)

Practice Test Two

True-False			Multiple Choice			
1.	T (p. 75)		1.	C (p. 69)	6.	A (p. 81)
2.	F (p. 81)		2.	B (p. 82)	7.	D (p. 81)
3.	T (p. 82)		3.	B (p. 75)	8.	B (p. 84)
4.	T (p. 84)		4.	D (p. 83)	9.	B (p. 85)
5.	T (p. 90)		5.	A (p. 83)	10.	D (p. 86)

APPLICATIONS/EXERCISES/ACTIVITIES

1.   How is affirmative action changing? Why is it a highly controversial public issue and what are the current affirmative action issues in the United States? Go to the following web site for the latest information on this topic: http://www.diverseeducation.com/artman/publish/article_6765.shtml

2.   How closely does the college faculty at your college or university reflect the city, state, and nation's racial composition? What about for males versus females? Are there any distinctions made by academic rank?

Chapter 3 – Discrimination

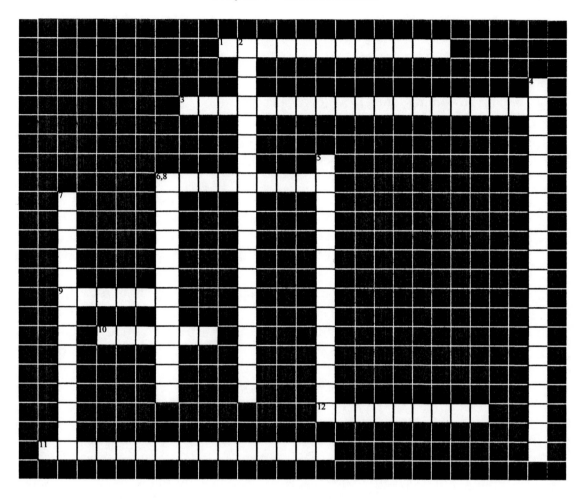

Across:

1   The principle that holds that each state is sovereign and has the right to order its own affairs without interference by the federal government

3   The conscious experience of a negative discrepancy between legitimate expectations and present actualities

6   A barrier to moving laterally in a business to positions that are more likely to lead to upward mobility

9   Salaries, wages, and other money received

10   An inclusive term encompassing all of a person's material assets, including land and other types of property

11   Transfers of money, goods, or services that are not reported to the government

12   The pattern of discrimination against people trying to buy homes in minority and racially changing neighborhoods

Down:

2   The combination of current discrimination with past discrimination created by poor schools and menial jobs

4   Efforts to ensure that hazardous substances are controlled so that all communities receive protection regardless of race or socioeconomic circumstances

5   The male advantage experienced in occupation dominated by women

7   The denial of opportunities and equal rights to individuals and groups because of prejudice or for other arbitrary reasons

8   The barrier that blocks the promotion of a qualified worker because of gender or minority membership

Chapter Four

Immigration and the United States

CHAPTER OBJECTIVES
- To learn how immigration is a global phenomenon
- To learn about the history and patterns of immigration to the United States
- To understand about today's foreign-born population in the United States
- To understand and evaluate the evolution of laws concerning immigration to the United States
- To learn about and question common stereotypes about immigrants
- To explore and evaluate contemporary social concerns with immigrants today
- To explore the distinction between legal and illegal immigration, the roles that immigrants play in the U.S. economy and what our society would be like without illegal immigrants
- To evaluate and understand the economic impact of immigration in the United States
- To understand the issues surrounding and facing women and immigration
- To understand the impact of the global economy and the role of immigration worldwide
- To understand the government's policy toward refugees and asylees

CHAPTER OUTLINE
I.   Immigration: A Global Phenomenon
- Immigration is a world wide phenomenon and contributes to globalization as more and more people see the world as their "home" rather than one specific country. An important factor contributing to immigration anywhere is *chain immigration,* an immigrant who sponsors several other immigrants who upon their arrival may sponsor still more.

II. Patterns of Immigration to the United States
- The diversity of ethnic and racial backgrounds of Americans today is the living legacy of immigration. While social forces that cause people to emigrate are complex, the most important have been economic. The reception given to immigrants in this country has not always been friendly. Opinion polls in the United States from 1965 through 2002 have never shown more than fourteen percent of the public in favor of more immigration.

III. Today's Foreign-Born Population
- Among today's United States population, ten percent are foreign-born. This figure is between the high figure of fifteen percent in 1890 and a low of five percent in 1970. The majority of foreign-born people are from Latin America.

IV. Early Immigration
- The English accounted for sixty percent of the three million White Americans in 1790. Throughout American history, immigration policy has been politically controversial. Since the early 1900s, about thirty-five percent of immigrants to the United States have emigrated back to the nation of origin.
- *Xenophobia* is the fear or hatred of strangers or foreigners has since the founding of our nation led to *nativism*, or beliefs and policies favoring native-born citizens over immigrants. From independence until around 1820, little evidence appeared of the anti-Catholic sentiment of colonial days, but the cry against "popery" grew as Irish immigrants increased. By the 1850s, nativism became an open political movement pledged to vote only for "native" Americans, to fight Catholicism, and demand a 21-year naturalization period.
  A. The Anti-Chinese Movement
  - *Sinophobes* are people with a fear of anything associated with China. Before 1851, official records show that only forty-six Chinese had immigrated to the United States. By the early 1880s that number had surpassed 200,000. After the labor of the Chinese had been used to help built the cross-continental railroad, Chinese immigration was not welcomed at all.
  - In 1882, Congress enacted the Chinese Exclusion Act, which outlawed Chinese immigration for ten years. In 1892, Congress extended the Exclusion Act for another ten years.

V. Restrictionist Sentiment Increases
  A. The National Origin System
  - The national origin system was begun in 1921 and remained the basis of immigration policy until 1965. This system established quotas for how many from a country could enter the United States annually. The quotas were deliberately weighted in favor of immigration from northern Europe. By the end of the 1920s, annual immigration had dropped to one-fourth of its pre-World War I level.
  B. The 1965 Immigration and Naturalization Act
  - As reflected in the title of this act, it set down the rules for becoming a citizen. *Naturalization* is the conferring of citizenship on a person after birth. Five general rules are used to determine whether someone can become naturalized (p. 105).
  - Legal immigrants admitted to the United States, by region of last residence, is presented in *Figure 4.5* (p. 105). Overall, half of the immigrants come to join their relatives, one-fourth are admitted for their special skills, and another quarter enter because of special refugee status. Over the past roughly twenty years eighty-one percent of immigrants to the United States have come from Latin America or Asia.

VI.   Contemporary Concerns
    A.   The Brain Drain
        • The *brain drain* is the immigration to the United States of skilled workers, professionals, and technicians who are desperately needed by their home countries. Conflict theorists see the current brain drain as yet another symptom of the unequal distribution of world resources.
    B.   Population Growth
        • Legal immigration accounted for twenty-five percent of the nation's growth in the 1990s. Other countries do have higher rates of immigration than the United States. There are distinctive patterns of uneven settlement patterns of immigrants in the United States.

VII.   Illegal Immigration
    • Immigrants are pulled here by lure of prosperity and better lives for their children, and they are pushed out of their native lands by unemployment and poverty. There are currently more than eight million illegal immigrants in the United States.
    • In the context of illegal immigration, Congress approved the Immigration Reform and Control Act of 1986. Amnesty was given to 1.7 million illegal immigrants who could document that they had established long-term residency in the United States. This act prohibited employers from discriminating against legal aliens because they were not citizens of the United States.
    • The 1996 Illegal Reform and Immigrant-Responsibility Act emphasized more effort to keep immigrants from entering the country by denying them access to various social welfare programs and benefits.
    • Listen to Our Voices: *The Wall That Keeps Illegal Works In*
    • Following 9/11, management of immigration in the United States was reorganized, as of March 1, 2003, from INS in the Department of Justice to three new agencies in the new Department of Homeland Security.

VIII.   The Economic Impact of Immigration
    • Social science studies generally contradict many of the negative stereotypes about the economic impact of immigration.
    • One economic aspect of immigration that has received increasing attention is the effort to measure *remittances* (or *migradollars*), or the monies that immigrants return to their country of origin.
    • States have sought legal redress because the federal government has not seriously considered granting impact aid to heavily burdened states. California's 1994 referendum, Proposition 187 illustrates this pattern.
    • Research Focus: *How Well Are Immigrants Doing?*

IX.   Women and Immigration
    • Immigration is presented as if all immigrants are similar with the only distinctions being made concerning point of origin, education, and employment prospects. The second-class status of women experience

normally in society is reflected in immigration. Immigration women, face all of the challenges faced by immigrant men plus some additional ones. Women play a critical role in overseeing the household and for immigrant women the added pressures of being in a new country and trying to move ahead is a different culture heighten this social role

X.   The Global Economy and Immigration
   • *Globalization* is the worldwide integration of government policies, cultures, social movements, and financial markets through trade, movement of people, and the exchange of ideas. *Transnationals* are immigrants who sustain multiple social relationships linking their societies of origin and settlement.
   A.   Refugees
      • *Refugees* are people living outside their country of citizenship for fear of political or religious persecution. There are some fifteen million refugees worldwide. The United States makes the largest financial contribution of any nation to worldwide assistance programs for refugees. The United States hosted a cumulative of about 1 million refugees between 1990 and 2003. Many nations much smaller and much poorer than the United States have many more refugees.

XI.   Conclusion
   • Immigration is the basis upon which the United States is based. Immigration policies and laws have dramatically affected immigration rates historically. There are many other social forces internal and external to the United States affecting immigration.

KEY TERMS

asylees (p. 119)

brain drain (p. 107)

chain immigration (p. 97)

globalization (p. 117)

nativism (p. 100)

naturalization (p. 105)

refugees (p. 118)

remittances (or migradollars) (p. 114)

sinophobes (p. 101)

transnationals (p. 118)

xenophobia (p. 100)

PRACTICE TESTS

Practice Test One

True-False

1.   T F   *Sinophobes* are people with a fear of anything associated with China.
2.   T F   In 1917 Congress enacted an immigration bill that opened immigration to Southern European and Asian nations.
3.   T F   After the passage of the Immigration and Naturalization Act of 1965, immigration declined by one-third compared to the first half of the twentieth century.
4.   T F   Overall, half of the immigrants come to the United States today to join their relatives.
5.   T F   Estimates are that there are fewer than one million illegal immigrants in the United States today.

Multiple Choice

1.   Two very different locales— _____ and _____ —are illustrated in the text to point out the different lives of immigrants in the United States.
      A. a professional football team in Ohio/a bakery in Indiana
      B. a taxi service in New York/a Hotel in Illinois
      C. an escort service in Boston/a modeling agency in Los Angeles.
      D. a California car repair shop/the governor's mansion in Iowa

2.   Which two decades in the history of the United States had the highest numbers of immigrants enter the country?
      A. 1900-1909 and 1990-1999
      B. 1820-1829 and 1930-1939
      C. 1970-1979 and 1980-1989
      D. 1840-1849 and 1920-1929

3.   The majority of today's twenty-eight million foreign-born people in the United States are from
      A. Asia
      B. Europe
      C. Central America
      D. the Caribbean

4.   In 1790 the _____ accounted for sixty percent of the three million White Americans.
      A. Germans
      B. English
      C. French
      D. Scottish

5. The national origin system was begun in _____ and remained the basis of immigration policy until _____.
   A. 1840-1869
   B. 1871-1917
   C. 1921-1965
   D. 1961-1990

6. The primary goals of the 1965 Immigration and Naturalization Act were to
   A. encourage immigration from Europe and give citizenship to current illegal immigrants.
   B. reduce the number of refuges coming to the United States and restrict remittances.
   C. restrict immigration from Latin America and limit illegal immigration.
   D. to reunite families and protect the American labor market.

7. Legal immigrants from Latin America and Asia accounted for _____ percent of all legal immigration to the United States between 1981-2000.
   A. 55
   B. 68
   C. 81
   D. 96

8. How many changes or amendments are there to the United States Constitution?
   A. 10
   B. 13
   C. 21
   D. 27

9. Immigrants who sustain multiple social relationships linking their societies of origin and settlement are:
   A. transnationals.
   B. refugees.
   C. asylees.
   D. globalites.

10. California's 1994 referendum, Proposition 187, symbolized the revolt against
    A. sweatshops.
    B. illegal immigration.
    C. the exploitation of migrant farm workers
    D. restrictive immigration policies.

Short-Answer Questions
1. Describe the general rules of the 1965 Immigration and Naturalization Act.
2. What social forces operated during the 1920 through the 1960s to influence the immigration policies and rates in the United States?
3. Describe the anti-Chinese movement of the late 1800s in the United States and its causes.
4. What was the national origin system? What were its effects on immigration to the United States?
5. Discuss the nature and the effects of the brain drain.

Practice Test Two

True-False
1. T F Opinion polls in the United States from 1965 through 2003 have never shown more than seventeen percent of the public in favor of more immigration.
2. T F *Nativism* encourages immigration.
3. T F In 1882, Congress enacted the Chinese Exclusion Act, which outlawed Chinese immigration for ten years.
4. T F During the 1920s, immigration rates increased by over fifty percent of its pre-World War I rates.
5. T F The United States has more *refugees* than any other nation in the world.

Multiple Choice
1. The first immigrant group to be singled out for restriction, with the passage of the 1882 Exclusion Act, were the _____.
   A. Chinese
   B. Mexicans
   C. Polish
   D. Irish

2. The social forces that cause people to emigrate are complex. The most important ones have been _____.
   A. religious
   B. economic
   C. environmental
   D. familial

3. The fear or hatred of strangers of foreigners refers to
   A. nativism
   B. ethnocentrism
   C. aggrephobia.
   D. xenophobia

4. The national origin system established in 1921 set the quota for each nation
    at ___ percent of the number of people descended from each nationality
    recorded in the 1920 census.
    A. 3
    B. 12
    C. 24
    D. 33

5. The *Listen to Our Voices* box entitled *"The Wall That Keeps Illegal Workers
    In"* discusses the idea that the United States needs an immigration policy that
    A. represses immigrants through unilaterial police action.
    B. seeks to manage the cross-border flows of people.
    C. is militarized.
    D. includes a wall built along the U.S.-Mexican border.

6. Between 1901 and 1940 seventy-nine percent of legal immigrants to the
    United States were from Europe. In between 1981-2000, the corresponding,
    figures for Europeans was ___ percent.
    A. less and 1
    B. 7
    C. 13
    D. 26

7. Legal immigration accounted for ___ percent of the population growth in the
    United States in the first years in the twenty-first century.
    A. 25
    B. 45-60
    C. 65
    D. 75

8. The target group of the national origin system of 1921 was
    A. Southern Europeans.
    B. Asians.
    C. Latin Americans.
    D. Indians (from India).

9. Remittances, or monies that immigrants return to their country of origin, are also
    known as
    A. globaldollars.
    B. transdollars.
    C. migradollars.
    D. natisitdollars.

10.   _____ is the worldwide integration of government policies, cultures, social movements, and financial markets through trade, movement of people, and exchange of ideas.
    A. Transnationalism
    B. Globalization
    C. Cross-culturalism
    D. Nativism

Short-Answer Questions
1.   What special challenges do women immigrants face? Be specific.
2.   Discuss the economic impact of immigration in the United States.
3.   What points are being made in the text concerning our government's policies and practices concerning *refugees?*
4.   Briefly discuss what happened as a result of Congress enacting the Chinese Exclusion Act in 1882.
5.   Describe the general demographic characteristics of our society's *foreign-born* population.

ANSWERS TO PRACTICE TEST QUESTIONS

Practice Test One

True-False		Multiple Choice			
1.	T (p. 101)	1.	D (p. 96)	6.	C (p. 104)
2.	F (p. 102)	2.	A (p. 99)	7.	C (p. 105)
3.	F (p. 104)	3.	C (p. 100)	8.	D (p. 106)
4.	T (p. 106)	4.	B (p. 100)	9.	A (p. 118)
5.	F (p. 109)	5.	C (p. 104)	10.	B (p. 116)

Practice Test Two

True-False		Multiple Choice			
1.	T (p. 98)	1.	A (p. 102)	6.	C (p. 105)
2.	F (pp. 100-101)	2.	B (p. 96)	7.	B (p. 108)
3.	T (p. 102)	3.	D (p. 100)	8.	A (p. 109)
4.	F (p. 104)	4.	A (p. 104)	9.	C (p. 114)
5.	F (p. 118)	5.	B (p. 110-111)	10.	B (p. 117)

APPLICATIONS/EXERCISES/ACTIVITIES

1. Locate the article "Statue of Liberty: The Shameful Story," from <u>Revolutionary Worker</u>, June 16, 1986. Read this very critical, but thought provoking, treatment of the United States' past immigration practices. Discuss in groups your reactions to this treatment.

2. Research the background of your own immigrant ancestors. What countries did they come from? How did they come? Did they come with people they knew? Where did they settle?

3. Take a trip to your local grocery store. Spend time walking down the aisle that stocks ethnic foods. Makes some notes about the degree to which you observe evidence of cultural stereotyping and ethnic-specific messages. In your analysis observe the packaging and type of ethnic good. Address factors such as placement in the store or the interest that other customers may have toward food. Give an oral report covering these issues:
    *   What were your first reactions? Are the foods different from those you recall from your youth?
    *   Did you find that some ethnic groups were more represented than other ethnic groups? If so, which one?
    *   How would you describe the ethnic foods? What were the most common types?
    *   Approximately what proportion of products in the grocery store are ethnically related?
    *   What would happen if multiculturalism became a more dominant ideology in our society? Would it change the type and amount of ethnic foods you would see in the grocery store?
    *   What did you learn about your society from this short exercise?

Chapter 4 – Immigration and the United States

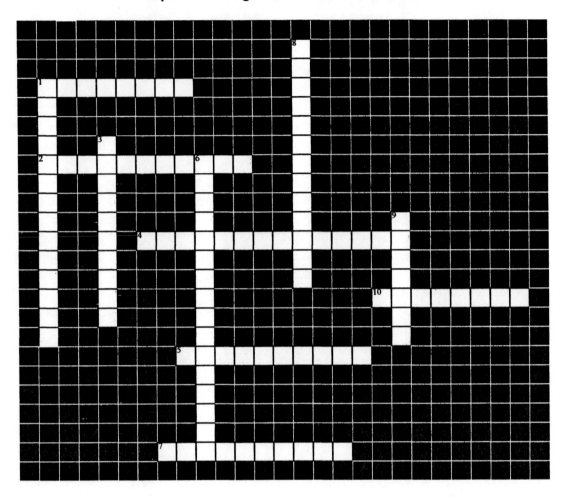

Across:
1   Beliefs and policies favoring native-born citizens over immigrants
2   (or migradollars) The monies that immigrants return to their country of origin
4   Immigrants who sustain multiple social relationships linking their societies of origin and settlement
5   Immigration to the United States of skilled workers, professionals, and technicians who are desperately needed by their home countries
7   The fear or hatred of strangers or foreigners
10   People living outside their country of citizenship for fear of political or religious persecution

Down:
1   Conferring of citizenship on a person after birth
3   People with a fear of anything associated with China
6   Immigrants sponsor several other immigrants who upon their arrival may sponsor still more
8   Worldwide integration of government policies, cultures, social movements, and financial markets through trade, movements of people, and the exchange of ideas
9   Foreigners who have already entered the United States and now seek protection because of persecution of a well-founded fear of persecution

Chapter Five

Ethnicity and Religion

CHAPTER OBJECTIVES
- To understand how religion and ethnicity contribute to defining identity
- To understand the idea of just what ethnicity is
- To understand the formation of Whiteness as an identity and the experiences of and the price paid by White ethnics in the United States
- To understand why researchers don't really study the concept of whiteness
- To understand and evaluate the different sociological perspectives regarding the origins and functions of ethnicity in the United States
- To understand and evaluate the experience of Irish Americans
- To understand and evaluate the experience of Italian Americans
- To understand and evaluate the experience of Polish Americans
- To learn about and evaluate issues surrounding the language divide
- To understand how race, religion, ethnicity, and social class may influence life chances
- To explore the similarities and differences in the United States by religion
- To evaluate and understand the limits of religious freedom using the Amish as an example

CHAPTER OUTLINE
I.   Ethnic Diversity
- The ethnic diversity of the United States at the beginning of the twenty-first century is apparent to almost everyone. Germans are the largest ancestral group, with one-fourth of Americans saying they had at least one German ancestor.

II.   Why Don't We Study Whiteness?
- Two aspects of White as a race are useful to consider: the historical creation of whiteness and how contemporary White people reflect on their racial identity.
  A.   Whiteness
  - Contemporary White Americans generally give little thought to "being White." Whites enjoy the privilege of not being reminded of their Whiteness.
  B.   White Privilege
  - Being White or being successful in establishing a White identity carries with it distinct advantages.
  C.   The Rediscovery of Ethnicity
  - *The Third-Generation Principle* is an early exception to the assimilationist approach to White ethnic groups. Simply stated—the grandchildren of the original immigrants—ethnic interest and awareness would actually increase.

D. Symbolic Ethnicity
- According to Herbert Gans, ethnicity today increasingly involves the symbols of ethnicity such as eating ethnic food, acknowledging ceremonial holidays, and supporting specific political issues or the issues confronting the old country. It does not include active involvement in ethnic activities or participation in ethnic-related organizations.
Ethnicity that does exist may be more a result of living in the United States than actual importing of practices from the past or the old country. Maintaining ethnicity can be a critical step toward successful assimilation. This is the *ethnic paradox.*

III. The Price Paid by White Ethnics
A. Prejudice toward White Ethnic Groups
Hostility toward White ethnics has been called *respectable bigotry.*
B. The Prejudice of Ethnics
- In the 1960s, as the civil rights movement moved north, White ethnics replaced the southern White as the typical bigot portrayed in the mass media. Evidence suggests minimal differences between ethnics and others in terms of prejudice.

IV. The Irish Americans
A. Early Irish Immigration
- The Protestants dominated the early Irish immigration to the colonies even though these Presbyterians from Ireland of Scotch descent accounted for only one out of ten. The Roman Catholics among the early immigrants were a diverse group.
B. The Famine Years
- This new migration fleeing the old country was much more likely to consist of families rather than single men. By the 1850s, nativism become an open political movement pledged to vote only for "native" Americans, to fight Catholicism, and to demand a twenty-one year naturalization period.
C. Becoming White
- Some 60,000 Irish signed an address in 1841 petitioning Irish Americans to join the abolitionist movement in the U.S. As Irish immigration continued, they began to see themselves favorably in comparison to the initial waves of Italian, Polish, and Slovak Roman Catholic immigrants.
D. Contemporary Irish Americans
- This immigration is relatively slight accounting for perhaps 1 out of 1000 legal arrivals today compared to over a third of all immigrants in the 1840s and 1850s. They were the first immigrant group to encounter prolonged organized resistance. They finally became an integral part of the United States.

V.   The Italian Americans
 •   Italian immigration was concentrated not only in time but also geography. The majority of the early Italian immigrants were landless peasants from southern Italy, the *mezzogiorno*. Many Italians during the nineteenth century received their jobs through an ethnic labor contractor, the *padrone*. Exploitation was common in the padrone system. Today, more than seventy percent of Italian Americans identify themselves as Roman Catholics.

VI. Polish Americans
 A.   Early Immigration
  •   They were among the settlers of Jamestown, Virginia in 1608 to help develop the colony's timber industry but it was the Poles that came later in that century that made a lasting mark.
 B.   Polonia
  •   *Polonia* (meaning Polish American communities) became more common in cities throughout the Midwest. Religion has played an important role for immigrants. The Jewish-Catholic distinction may be the most obvious distinguishing factor among Poles.
 C.   The Contemporary Picture
  •   Today Polonia numbers 9 million. Many Polish Americans have retained little of their rich cultural traditions and may barely acknowledge even symbolic ethnicity. In the latter part of the twentieth century some of the voluntary associations relocated or built satellite centers to serve the outlying Polish American populations.

VII. The Language Divide
 A.   Listen to Our Voices: I Was Born In Tirana
 B.   Bilingual Education
  •   *Bilingualism* is the use of two or more languages in places of work or education facilities, according each language equal legitimacy. A program of *bilingual education* may instruct children in their native language while gradually introducing them to the language of the dominant society. *English immersion* is teaching in English by teachers who know the students' native language but use it only when students do not understand the lesson.
 C.   Official Language Movement
  •   Attacks on bilingualism both in voting and in education have taken several forms and have even broadened to question the appropriateness of U.S. residents using any language other than English.

VIII. Religious Pluralism
 •   In 2004, it was estimated that the nation was eighty-six percent Christian, nearly seven percent non-religious, and about seven percent all other faiths.
 •   Sociologists use the term *denomination* for a large, organized religion that is not linked officially with the state or government. By far the largest religious denomination in the United States is Catholicism.

- One notable characteristic of religious practice in the United States is its segregated nature at the local level broadly defined, faiths show representation of a variety of ethnic and racial groups. About 2 out of 3 Americans are counted as church members, but it is difficult to assess the strength of their religious commitment.
- Sunday is still "the most segregated hour of the week."
A.   Research Focus: Measuring the Importance of Religion

IX.   Ethnicity, Religion, and Social Class
- Pioneer sociologist Max Weber described *life chances* as people's opportunities to provide themselves with material goods, positive living conditions, and favorable life experiences.
- Some studies have shown that ethnicity is more important than religion in explaining behavior.
- Social class is yet another factor. *Ethclass* combines the concepts of ethnicity and class denoting the importance of each.

X.   Religion in the United States
- *Civil religion* is the religious dimension American life that merges the state with sacred beliefs.
- Functionalists see civil religion as reinforcing Central American values that may be more expressly patriotic than sacred in nature.
A.   Diversity among Roman Catholics
  - The Roman Catholic Church, despite its ethnic diversity, has clearly been a powerful force in reducing the ethnic ties of its members, making it also a significant assimilating force.
B.   Diversity among Protestants
  - Four "generic theological camps" are identified: liberals, moderates, conservative, and fundamentalists.
  - Religious faiths may be distinguished by secular criteria as well as doctrinal issues.
  - Protestant faiths have been diversifying, and many members have been leaving them for churches that follow strict codes of behavior or fundamental interpretations of Biblical teachings.
  - Denominations vary considerably in terms of median income and in terms of the proportion of members with a college degree.
C.   Women and Religion
  - Religious beliefs have often placed women in an exalted but protected position. This often means being "protected" from becoming leaders. Despite these restrictions, there has been a notable rise in female clergy in the last twenty years.
D.   Religion and the U.S. Supreme Court
  - Religious pluralism owes its existence in the United States to the First Amendment. The United States Supreme Court has consistently interpreted its wording to mean not that government should ignore religion but that it should follow a policy of neutrality to maximize religious freedom.

- Several religious groups have been in legal and social conflict with the rest of society. Some can be called *secessionist minorities*, in that they reject both assimilation and coexistence in some form of cultural pluralism.
- *Creationists*, or people who support the literal interpretation of the Bible, have formed various organizations to crusade for creationist treatment in American public schools and universities.
- Issues surrounding religious rituals are also being discussed in the Supreme Court.
- The battle over public displays that depict symbols of or seem associated with a religion are currently being argued in the Supreme Court.

XI.   Limits of Religious Freedom: The Amish
- By 2003, there were about 1,400 Old Order Amish settlements in the United States and Canada. Estimates place membership at about 180,000, with approximately seventy-five percent living in three states: Pennsylvania, Ohio, and Indiana.
- The Amish practice self-segregation, living in settlements divided into church districts that are autonomous congregations composed of about seventy-five baptized members.
- The Amish practice *Meidung*, or shunning; the social norms of this secessionist minority that have evolved over the years are known as *Ordnung*.
- The Amish do not totally reject social change. More and more Amish are becoming entrepreneurs and such occupations sometimes become a source of tension with the larger society. Stratification is largely absent in Amish society.
- The Old Order Amish have developed a pluralistic position that has become increasingly difficult to maintain as their numbers grow and as they enter the economy in competition with the English, or non-Amish.

KEY TERMS

civil religion (p. 152)	bilingual education (p. 143)	English immersion (p.144)
creationists (p. 158)	bilingualism (p. 143)	life chances (p. 151)
denomination (p. 147)	respectable bigotry (p. 130)	ethclass (p. 152)
ethnicity paradox (p. 129)	symbolic ethnicity (p. 128)	secessionist minority (p. 158)
intelligence design (p. 159)	principle of third-generation interest (p. 127)	

PRACTICE TESTS

Practice Test One

True-False
1.   T F   Germans are the largest ancestral group in the United States.
2.   T F   About thirty percent of adults in the United States identify themselves as *nonreligious.*
3.   T F   The immigration of Italians was enhanced by the *national origin system.*
4.   T F   Religious faiths may be distinguished by secular criteria as well as doctrinal issues.
5.   T F   Seventy-five percent of the Amish live in three states: Pennsylvania, Ohio, and Indiana.

Multiple Choice
1. In the Listen to Our Voices box entitled "I Was Born in Tirana" the author speaks out about his efforts to attend
   A. Johnson College
   B. Truman College
   C. Roosevelt College
   D. Lincoln College

2. In popular speech, the term *pluralism* has often been used in the United States to refer explicitly to _____.
   A. race
   B. age
   C. social class
   D. religion

3. The *principle of third-generation interest*
   A. takes an assimilationist approach.
   B. maintains that ethnic interest and awareness increases from the first to the third generation of immigrants.
   C. suggests economic opportunity and popular culture diminishes ethnic significance in our society within three generations.
   D. None of the above.

4. Approximately what percentage of Americans say that religion is very important in their lives?
   A. 20
   B. 40
   C. 60
   D. 80

5.   The *ethnicity paradox* suggests
     A. ethnicity can be a critical step toward successful assimilation.
     B. the longer an ethnic group has lived in the United States the less integrated into society they seem to be.
     C. White ethnics suffer harsher discrimination today than do racial minorities.
     D. None of the above.

6.   The Catholic Church was dominated early in America by which immigrant group?
     A. Italians
     B. Irish
     C. Spanish
     D. French

7.   Research by Andrew Greeley illustrated that
     A. religion was stronger than ethnicity in predicting attitudes and behaviors.
     B. ethnicity was stronger than religion in predicting attitudes and behaviors.
     C. Catholics are more religious in their attitudes and behaviors than Protestants.
     D. social class had little association with religious identification.

8.   _____ see civil religion as reinforcing central Americans values that may be more expressly patriotic than sacred in nature.
     A. Conflict theorists
     B. Symbolic-interactionists
     C. Exchange theorists
     D. Functionalists

9.   Which of the following denominations has the highest percentage of followers who have a *college degree*?
     A. Catholic
     B. Presbyterian
     C. Jewish
     D. Mormon

10. The social norms of the Amish that have evolved over the years are known as
     A. Yodernund.
     B. Ordnung.
     C. Festivus.
     D. Meidung.

Short-Answer Questions

1. What is meant by the idea the Whites enjoy the privilege of not being reminded of their whiteness?
2. What is the evidence, in your opinion, that religion is largely absent from television?
3. What is meant by the term *respectable bigotry*?
4. Describe the diversity among Protestants in the United States today.
5. What have been important decisions made by the United States Supreme Court that have impacted religious pluralism in our society?

Practice Test Two

True-False

1. T F By far the largest denomination in the United States is Catholicism.
2. T F One notable characteristic of religious practice in the United States is its segregated nature.
3. T F Most Jehovah Witnesses in the United States are Black.
4. T F Between 1980 and 2001 the percentage of Americans saying that "religion is very important in my life" has decreased dramatically.
5. T F Research has consistently shown that denomination can be arranged in a hierarchy based on social class.

Multiple Choice

1. It is estimated that in 2005 the United States was _____ Christian.
    A. 30
    B. 54
    C. 82
    D. 94

2. Which of the following religious groups has the highest percentage of its members identifying themselves as "White."
    A. Roman Catholics
    B. Seventh Day Adventists
    C. Baptists
    D. Lutherans

3. "What the son wishes to forget the grandson wishes to remember" is a saying that reflects
    A. the ethnic paradox.
    B. the principle of third-generation interest.
    C. the respectable bigotry principle.
    D. the essence of symbolic ethnicity.

4.   Hostility toward _____ is sometimes referred to as *respectable bigotry*.
     A. religious people
     B. third-generation ethnics
     C. White ethnics
     D. symbolic ethnicity

5.   The *Columbian Coalition*, founded in 1971, employs lawyers to handle cases of _____ Americans who claim they are victims of bigotry.
     A. Italian
     B. Irish
     C. Protestant
     D. Spanish

6.   The *Padrone system* was found among which ethnic group?
     A. Jewish
     B. Irish
     C. Italian
     D. Polish

7.   _____ religion is a religious dimension in American life that merges the state with sacred beliefs.
     A. Ethclass
     B. Civil
     C. State
     D. Nondenominational

8.   The Roman Catholic Church, despite ethnic diversity, has been a clearly powerful force in creating _____.
     A. segregation
     B. secessionism
     C. stratification
     D. assimilation

9.   Which of the following denominations has the *lowest median income*?
     A. Jewish
     B. Catholic
     C. Baptist
     D. Presbyterian

10. The 1962 Supreme Court case decision in *Engel v. Vitale* dealt with
     A. prayer in school.
     B. secessionist minorities.
     C. respectable bigotry.
     D. religion in the media.

Short-Answer Questions

1.   Briefly explain the *principle of third-generation interest*.
2.   What is meant by the term *symbolic ethnicity*?
3.   Briefly describe diversity among Roman Catholics.
4.   Explain how the Amish represent a *secessionist minority*.
5.   What is meant by the term *ethnicity paradox*?

ANSWERS TO PRACTICT TEST QUESTIONS

Practice Test One

True-False

1.	T (p. 124)
2.	F (p. 146)
3.	F (p. 137)
4.	T (p. 154)
5.	T (p. 159)

Multiple Choice

1.	B (p. 142)	6.	B. (p. 136)
2.	D (p. 146)	7.	B (p. 152)
3.	B (p. 127)	8.	D (p. 152)
4.	C (p. 154)	9.	C (p. 155)
5.	A (p. 129)	10.	B (p. 160)

Practice Test Two

True-False

1.	T (p. 148)
2.	T (p. 147)
3.	F (p. 149)
4.	F (p. 151)
5.	T (p. 154)

Multiple Choice

1.	C (p. 146)	6.	C (p. 136)
2.	D (p. 148)	7.	B (p. 152)
3.	B (p. 127)	8.	D (p. 153)
4.	C (p. 130)	9.	C (p. 155)
5.	A (p. 130)	10.	A (p. 157)

APPLICATIONS/EXERCISES/ACTIVITIES

1.   During World War II, Italian-Americans were placed in internment camps in the United States. What restrictions and exclusions did Italian-Americans face during this period of time? Why were these internment campus created? Visit Una Storia Segreta: When Italian-Americans Were "Enemy Aliens," at http://hcom.csumb.edu/segreta/

2.   Attend, if practical, the services of an ethnically or nonwhite racially dominated church. What differences and similarities are there when compared to a church in a White middle-class neighborhood?

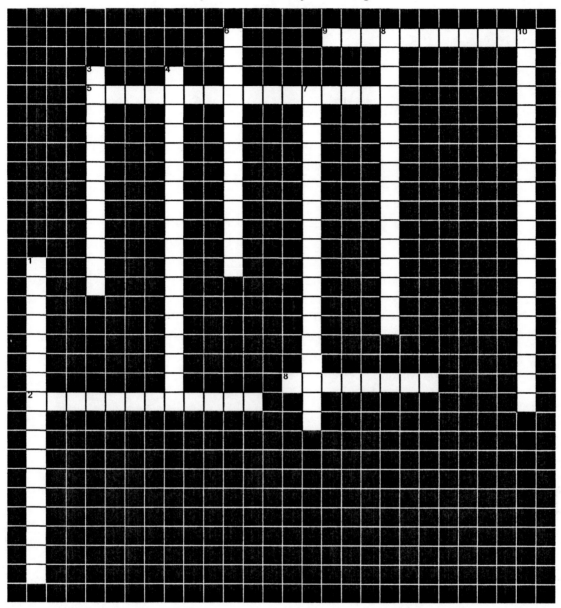

Across:

2 People who support a literal interpretation of the biblical account of the creation of the universe

5 Teaching in English by teachers who know the students' native language but use it only when students do not understand the lessons

8 The merged ethnicity and class in a person's status

9 People's opportunities to provide themselves with material goods, positive living conditions, and favorable life experiences

Down:

1 The idea that describes an emphasis on ethnic food and ethnically associated political issues rather than deeper ties to one's heritage

3 A large, organized religion not officially linked with the state or government

4 A program designed to allow students to learn academic concepts in their native language while they learn a second language

6 The religious dimension in American life that merges the state with sacred beliefs

7 The social acceptance of prejudice against White ethnics, when intolerance against non-White minorities is regarded as unacceptable

8 The maintenance of one's ethnic ties in a way that can assist with assimilation in larger society

10 Groups, such as the Amish that reject both assimilation and coexistence

Chapter Six

The Native Americans

CHAPTER OBJECTIVES
- To learn about the historical interactions between Europeans and Native Americans
- To learn about and evaluate the history of legislation targeting Native Americans especially concerning treaties and warfare
- To understand and evaluate the different methods that the federal government used to rule the Native Americans
- To learn how federal policies affect life on the reservation
- To understand and evaluate collective action efforts through pan-Indianism and protest efforts
- To learn about pan-Indianism and how contemporary Native Americans address issues of economic development, education, health care, religious and spiritual expression, and the environment
- To understand and explore the role of sovereignty in Native American tribal self-rule
- To evaluate the Native American Legal Claims, the Termination Act, and the Employment Assistance Program
- To understand and evaluate the Navajo way

CHAPTER OUTLINE
I. Early European Contacts
- In 1500, an estimated 700 distinct languages were spoken in the area north of Mexico. The number of Native Americans north of the Rio Grande was estimated to be about 10 million. The 2000 Census showed that there were approximately 2.5 million Native Americans in the United States, a thirty-two percent increase from 1990.
- The *world systems theory* takes the view that the global economic system is divided between nations that control wealth and those that provide natural resources and labor.

II. Treaties and Warfare
- Federal relations with the Native Americans were the responsibility of the Secretary of War. The bureau of Indian Affairs, created in 1824, was therefore part of the War Department.
- The Indian Removal Act, passed in 1830, called for the relocation of all Eastern tribes across the Mississippi.
  - A. The Case of the Sioux
    - The United States signed the Fort Laramie Treaty of 1868 with the Sioux, then under the leadership of Red Cloud. It formed the Great Sioux Reservation, which included all the land that is now South Dakota west of the Missouri River. White settlers continued to pour

into the region. In 1876, the Sioux reluctantly sold the Black Hills and agreed to the reduction of the Great Sioux Reservation.

- The Battle of the Little Big Horn, under the leadership of Crazy Horse, was the last great Sioux victory.
- The Ghost Dance (*a millenarian movement*) was a religion that included dances and songs proclaiming the return of the buffalo and the resurrection of dead ancestors in a land free of White people. A large Ghost Dance at Wounded Knee Creek on the Pine Ridge, South Dakota reservation in late December 1890 attracted the concern of a cavalry division. While attempting to disarm warrior dances a random shot was fired, touching off a massacre.

III. Ruling the Native Americans
- The government's intention to merge the various tribes into White society was unmistakably demonstrated in the 1887 Dawes, or General Allotment Act.

A. The Allotment Act
- The Allotment Act bypassed tribal leaders and proposed to make individual landowners of tribal members. Each family was given up to 160 acres. The effect of the Allotment Act on Native Americans was disastrous. Much of the land initially deeded under the Allotment Act wound up in the hands of Whites. The Bureau of Indian Affairs required that upon the death of the land owner, the land had to be equally divided among all descendents, regardless of tribal customs.

B. The Reorganization Act
- The Indian Reorganization Act of 1934, known as the Wheeler-Howard Act, recognized the need to use, rather than ignore, tribal identity. But assimilation, rather than movement toward a pluralistic society, was the goal.

IV. Reservation Life and Federal Policies
- Today, about 530,000 Native Americans live on 557 reservations and trust lands in 33 states, which account for a bit more than 2 percent of the land throughout the United States.

A. Native American Legal Claims
- From 1863 to 1946, Native Americans could bring no claim against the government without a special act of Congress. In 1946, Congress created the Indian Claims Commission, with authority to hear all tribal cases against the government. *Setoffs*, or deductions of monies for federal services, often took all the claimant's settlements.

B. The Termination Act
- The Termination Act of 1953 was the most controversial government policy toward reservation Native Americans during the twentieth century. The goals of the Act were to provide greater autonomy to Native Americans and also reduce government expenditures. Much of what occurred merely translated into a reduction in services for Native Americans living on reservations.

C.   Employment Assistance Program
- In 1952, the Bureau of Indian Affairs began programs to relocate young Native Americans. The EAPs primary provision was for relocation, individually or in families, at government expense, to urban areas where job opportunities were greater than those on reservations. The program had many unintended negative consequences.

V.   Collective Action
- The growth of pan-Indian activism is an example of both panethnicity and social protest. *Pan-Indianism* refers to intertribal social movements in which several tribes, joined by political goals but not by kinship, unite in a common identity. Proponents of this movement see tribes as captive nations or internal colonies.
- The National Congress of American Indians, founded in 1944 in Denver, Colorado, was the first national organization representing Native Americans. A more recent arrival is the more radical American Indian Movement, the most visible pan-Indian group.

A.   Protest Efforts
- *Fish-ins* began in 1964 to protest interference by Washington State officials with Native Americans who were fishing, as they argued, in accordance with the 1854 Treaty of Medicine Creek and were not subject to fine or imprisonment, even if they violate White society's law.
- In 1969, members of the San Francisco Indian Center seized Alcatraz Island in San Francisco Bay
- The Native Claims Settlement Act of 1971 was one of the most reasonable agreements reached between distinctive tribal groups of Native Americans and the government. This Act granted control and ownership of 44 million acres to Alaska's 53,000 Inuits.
- The occupation of the Pine Ridge reservation in South Dakota by member of the IAM in 1973 became known as Wounded Knee II. Recently AIM activity has been in efforts to gain clemency for one of its leaders, Leonard Peltier.

B.   Pan-Indianism: An Overview
- Pan-Indianism, an example of panethnicity, has created solidarity among Native Americans as they seek solutions to common grievances with government agencies.
- Not all results of pan-Indianism have been productive. The national organizations are dominated by Plains tribes both politically and culturally.
- Over the last hundred years, *powwows* have evolved into gatherings in which Native Americans of many tribes come to dance, sing, play music, and visit.

VI.   Sovereignty
- Although the collective gathering of tribes in pan-Indian efforts cannot be minimized, there continues to be a strong effort to maintain tribal *sovereignty*

(Tribal self-rule).

- Focused on the tribal group, sovereignty remains linked to both the actions of the federal government and the actions of individual American Indians.
- The federal government takes this gate keeping role of sovereignty very seriously--the irony of the conquering people determining who are "Indians" is not lost upon many tribal activists.
- Individual American Indians play a role as well

VII. Native Americans Today
    A. Economic Development
- The Native Americans are an impoverished people. They have higher poverty rates and lower incomes than other subordinate groups in our society. Native Americans differ in three areas from other racial and ethnic minorities in the United States: tourism, casino gambling, and government employment.

    B. Education
- Government involvement in the education of Native Americans dates as far back as a 1794 treaty with the Oneida Indians. Federal control of the education of Native American children has had mixed results from the beginning.
- A serious problem with Native American education has been the unusually high level of under-enrollment. The concepts *kickout* or *pushout* are meant to indicate that children are not so much hostile to education as they are set apart from it.
- The quality of Native American education is more difficult to measure than is the quantity. The *crossover effect* appears when tests used assume lifelong familiarity with English.
- The picture for Native Americans in higher education is decidedly mixed, with some progress and some promise. One encouraging development in higher education in recent years has been the creation of tribally controlled colleges, usually 2-year community colleges.
- Until the 1960s, BIA and mission schools forbade the speaking in the native languages.

    C. Research Focus: Learning the Navajo Way
    D. Health Care
- Native Americans have dramatic health problems compared to other groups in our society because of high rates of poverty and lack of health services.
- With the pressure to assimilate Native Americans in all aspects of their lives, there has been little willingness to recognize their traditions of healing and treating illnesses.

    E. Religious and Spiritual Expression
- Like other aspects of Native Americans culture, the expression of religion is diverse.
- In 1978 Congress enacted the American Indian Religious Freedom Act, which declares that it is the government's policy to "protect and preserve

the inherent right of American Indians to believe, express, and practice their traditional religions."

- In 1994, Congress amended the American Religious Freedom Act to allow Native Americans the right to use, transport, and possesses peyote for religious purposes.
- An area of spiritual concern is the stockpiling of Native American relics.

F.   Listen to Our Voices: The Scalpel and the Silver Bear
G.   Environment
- Environmental issues bring together many of the concerns we have previously considered surrounding Native Americans: land rights, environmental justice, economic development, and spiritualism.

KEY TERMS

crossover effect (p. 188)	pan-Indianism (p. 178)
environmental justice (p. 194)	powwows (p. 181)
fish-ins (p. 178)	world systems theory (p. 168)
internal colonialism (p. 172)	kickouts or pushouts (p. 187)
millenarian movements (p. 171)	

PRACTICE TESTS

Practice Test One

True-False

1.   T F   The number of Native Americans north of the Rio Grande was estimated to probably be about forty-five million in 1500.
2.   T F   *Indian reservations* account for about ten percent of the land throughout the United States.
3.   T F   The school dropout rate for Native Americans is at least fifty percent higher than that of Blacks and Hispanics.
4.   T F   In 1994 Congress amended the American Indian Religious Freedom Act to allow Native Americans the right to use, transport, and possess *peyote* for religious purposes.
5.   T F   According to the author of the text, environmental issues reinforce the tendency to treat the first inhabitants of the Americas as *inferior*.

Multiple Choice

1. In 1500, and estimated ____ *distinct languages* were spoken in the area north of Mexico.
    A. 200
    B. 300
    C. 500
    D. 700

2. The Bureau of Indian Affairs was established in 1824 and was part of the Department of
    A. Labor.
    B. State.
    C. War.
    D. Interior.

3. The Sioux victory over Custer's troops in the Battle of the Little Big Horn was under the leadership of
    A. Crazy Horse.
    B. Red Cloud.
    C. Sitting Bull.
    D. Chief Joseph.

4. At the heart of the *millenarian movement* was the _____ *dance.*
    A. River
    B. Ghost
    C. Buffalo
    D. Wolfe

5. Today, there are about 1.3 million Native Americans living on _____ *reservations.*
    A. 93
    B. 198
    C. 248
    D. 557

6. The *Corbell* case illustrates
    A. Native American legal claims.
    B. a percentage of Indian casino profits that must go to the federal government.
    C. Native Americans who have chosen not to live on reservations.
    D. monies set aside for Native Americans to buy land.

7.   This policy proposed to give Native Americans greater autonomy and at the same time reduce federal expenditures:
        A. the Termination Act
        B. Allotment Act
        C. Reorganization Act
        D. Indian Reform Act

8.   The *Native Claims Act of 1971* dealt with
        A. casinos in Michigan.
        B. land in Alaska.
        C. waterways in Maine.
        D. hunting in Wisconsin.

9.   The concept of *Powwow* is derived from the Algonquian term pau wau, meaning
        A. war party.
        B. sacred land.
        C. kinship.
        D. medicine man.

10.   The pattern of low-wage employment among Native Americans is typical of many racial and ethnic minority groups in the United States. But, Native Americans differ in three areas. Which of the following was not identified in the text of one of the areas?
        A. tourism
        B. casino gambling
        C. government employment
        D. family businesses

Short Answer Questions
1.   Describe the basic perspective being offered by proponents of *world systems theory*.
2.   What was the *Indian Removal Act* of 1830? What was its impact on Native Americans?
3.   Describe the treatment of the Sioux by the federal government during the nineteenth century.
4.   Provide two illustrations of *Pan-Indianism* as a means toward effective collective action.
5.   In what important ways has the government impacted the religious and spiritual expression of Native Americans?

Practice Test Two

True-False
1. T F Today, there are approximately one-hundred and fifty surviving Native American languages.
2. T F Probably the most successful government intervention into Native American affairs was the *General Allotment Act*, which proposed to make individual landowners of tribal members.
3. T F The National Congress of American Indians, founded in 1944 in Denver, Colorado, was the first national organization representing Native Americans.
4. T F Less than one-in-ten employees of the Bureau of Indian Affairs is Native American.
5. T F Today's Native Americans are asking that their traditions be recognized as an expression of pluralist rather than assimilationist coexistence.

Multiple Choice
1. _____ *theory* takes the view that the global economic system is divided between nations that control wealth and those that provide natural resources and labor.
   A. Developmental
   B. World systems
   C. Redistribution
   D. Resource

2. The Indian Removal Act in 1830, called for the relocation of
   A. all Eastern tribes across the Mississippi.
   B. all tribes in New England to South Dakota.
   C. all Plains Indians to reservations.
   D. None of the above.

3. The *millenarian movement* originated among the
   A. Iroquois.
   B. Cherokee.
   C. Paiutes.
   D. Creek.

4. In which state did the Battle of Wounded Knee take place?
   A. South Dakota
   B. Nebraska
   C. Wyoming
   D. Montana

5. The _____ of 1934 recognized the need to use, rather than ignore, tribal identity.
   A. Allotment Act
   B. Plains Act
   C. Termination Act
   D. Indian Reorganization Act

6. From ____ to ____, Native Americans could bring no claim against the government without a special act of Congress.
   A. 1789/1865
   B. 1783/1924
   C. 1863/1946
   D. 1924/1977

7. The _____ primary provision was for relocation, individually or in families, at government expense.
   A. Employment Assistance Program's
   B. Allotment Act's
   C. Termination Act's
   D. American Indian Movement's

8. The largest Native American tribal group in the United States is the
   A. Iroquois.
   B. Apache.
   C. Sioux.
   D. Cherokee.

9. Which of the following cities has the largest number of Native American residents?
   A. Los Angeles
   B. New York City
   C. Boston
   D. Seattle

10. The *cross-over effect* related to which of the following social institutions?
    A. education
    B. politics
    C. the economy
    D. religion

Short Answer Questions

1. Differentiate between the *Allotment Act* and the *Reorganization Act*. What impact did each have on Native Americans?
2. Identify four of the major failures in our society's effort to improve the education of Native Americans.
3. What are the four ways in which environmental literature has trivialized native cultures?
4. In what three ways do Native Americans differ from other minority groups in terms of *economic development*? Explain.
5. Describe the early European contact with Native Americans.

ANSWERS TO PRACTICE TEST QUESTIONS

Practice Test One

True-False		Multiple Choice			
1	F (p. 168)	1.	D (p. 167)	6.	A (p. 175)
2	F (p. 174)	2.	C (p. 169)	7.	A (p. 176)
3	T (p. 187)	3.	A (p. 170)	8.	B (p. 179)
4	T (p. 193)	4.	B (p. 171)	9.	D (p. 181)
5	T (p. 194)	5.	D (p. 174)	10.	D (p. 183)

Practice Test Two

True-False		Multiple Choice			
1	T (p. 168)	1.	B (p. 168)	6.	C (p. 175)
2	F (p. 172)	2.	A (p. 170)	7.	A (p. 177)
3	T (p. 178)	3.	C (p. 171)	8.	D (p. 180)
4	F (p. 185)	4.	A (p. 171)	9.	B (p. 182)
5	T (p. 194)	5.	D (p. 173)	10.	A (p. 188)

APPLICATIONS/EXERCISES/ACTIVITIES

1. Find information about three Native American groups at the following web site and indicate the differences in their lifestyles that emanate from their cultural histories. Go to: http://dir.yahoo.com/Regional/Countries/United_States/Society_and_Culture/Cult ures_and_Groups/Cultures/American__United_States_/Native_American/Tribes_ _Nations__and_Bands/

2. Read about the relationship between Native Americans and anthropologists. This issue has come more to light as some of the nation's leading museums have begin to return Native American relics and artifacts back to tribes. An historical look of this relationship is presented in the article, "Are Anthropologists Hazardous to Indians' Health?" in the *Journal of Ethnic Studies*, 15: 1- 38

Chapter 6 – The Native Americans

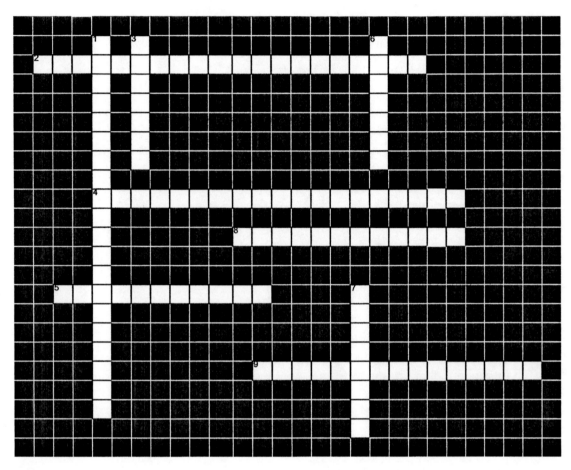

Across:

2   Efforts to ensure that hazardous substances are controlled so that all communities receive protection regardless of race or socioeconomic circumstances

4   The treatment of subordinate peoples as colonial subjects by those in power

5   Tribal self-rule

8   Intertribal social movements in which several tribes, joined by political goals but not by kinship, unite in a common identity

9   An effect that appears as previously high-scoring Native American children score as below average in intelligence when tests are given in English rather than their native languages

Down:

1   For example, the Ghost Dance, that prophesies a cataclysm in the immediate future, to be followed by collective salvation

3   Native American gatherings of dancing, singing, music playing, and visiting, accompanied by competitions

6   Tribes' protests over governmental interference with their traditional rights to fish as they like

7   Native American school dropouts who leave behind an unproductive academic environment

Chapter Seven

The Making of African Americans in a White America

CHAPTER OBJECTIVES

- To understand that the African presence in the United States began almost simultaneously with permanent White settlement
- To understand and evaluate the origins of slavery and its continuing impact on Black-White relations
- To broaden your understanding and evaluate the history of African Americans in early American history
- To explore and understand the challenge of Black leadership after the demise of slavery
- To understand and evaluate the role of Booker T. Washington and W.E.B. Du Bois in their role as American leaders as it pertains to the institutionalization of White supremacy after the demise of slavery
- To understand the reemergence of Black protest and the causes and nature of protest movements against racial inequality in this country
- To understand and evaluate the Civil Rights Movement
- To evaluate the situations of urban violence and oppression concerning African Americans in this country
- To understand and explore the role of Black Power and its approach to solving racial inequality
- To understand the diversity of African American leaders' approaches to the problem of racial inequality
- To evaluate and understand the role of religion in the struggle for racial equality in the United States
- To broaden your understanding of the long history of Sundown Towns where non-whites could work and spend their money but not live

CHAPTER OUTINE
I.   Slavery
     A.   Slave Codes
- Slavery in the United States rested on five central conditions: slavery was for life, the status was inherited, slaves were considered mere property, slaves were denied rights, and coercion was used to maintain the system.
- *Slave codes* were laws that defined the low position of slaves in the United States. Thirteen of the more common features of slave codes are identified on page 202.
- The slave family had no standing in law. Marriages between slaves were not legally recognized.

- Unlike the family structure, to which slavery dealt near-mortal blows, a strong religious tradition survived.
  B. African Americans and Africa
  - The survival of African culture can be most easily documented in folklore, religion, language, and music.
  - Research has identified remnants of grammar and sentence construction in the speech patterns of low-income and rural Blacks. *Ebonics* is the distinctive dialect, with a complex language structure, that is found among Black Americans.
  C. The Attack on Slavery
  - Antislavery advocates, or *abolitionists*, included both Whites and Blacks. The Constitution dealt the antislavery movement a blow. To appease the South, the framers of the Constitution recognized and legitimated slavery's existence.
  - Harriet Tubman, along with other Blacks and sympathetic Whites, developed the Underground Railroad to convey escaping slaves to freedom in the North and Canada.
  D. Slavery's Aftermath
  - On January 1, 1863, President Lincoln issued the Emancipation Proclamation. Six months after the surrender of the Confederacy in 1865, abolition became law when the Thirteenth Amendment abolished slavery throughout the nation.
  - From 1867 to 1877, during the period called Reconstruction, Black-White relations in the South were unlike anything they had ever been. In 1870, the Fifteenth Amendment was ratified, prohibiting the denial of the right to vote on the grounds of race, color, or previous condition of servitude.
  - Reconstruction was ended as part of a political compromise in the election of 1876, and, consequently became entrenched in the South.
  - In 1896, the United States Supreme Court ruled in *Plessy v. Ferguson* that state laws requiring "separate but equal" accommodations for Blacks were a "reasonable" use of state government power.
  E. Reparations for Slavery
  - *Slavery reparations* refers to the act of making amends for the injustice of slavery. There has not been an official government apology for slavery. Government policy makers for the most part have not been willing to endorse the concept of slave reparations in any way.

II. The Challenge of Black Leadership
  A. The Politics of Accommodation
  - Booker T. Washington's approach to White supremacy is called the politics of accommodation. His essential theme was compromise.
  B. The Niagara Movement
  - W.E.B. Du Bois was critical of Washington's statements that seemed to encourage Whites to place the burden of the Black's problems on the Blacks themselves.

- Du Bois thought education for African Americans should emphasize academics.
- Meetings at Niagara Falls placed the responsibility for problems facing Blacks on the shoulders of Whites.
- In 1910 the NAACP was founded by the Niagara Movement.

III.   Reemergence of Black Protest
- Racial turmoil during World War II included threatened marches for employment opportunities and racial disturbances in cities throughout the country.
- The war years and the postwar period saw several United States Supreme Court decisions that suggested the Court was moving away from tolerating racial inequalities.
- A *restrictive covenant* was a private contract entered into by neighborhood property owners stipulating that property could not be sold or rented to certain minority groups. In 1948 the Supreme Court finally declared restrictive covenants unconstitutional.
    A.   Research Focus: Sundown Towns, USA

IV.   The Civil Rights Movement
    A.   Struggle to Desegregate the Schools
- It is difficult to say exactly when a social movement begins or end. The author suggests though that the Civil Rights movement began with the United States Supreme Court decision in *Brown v. Board of Education of Topeka, Kansas.* This ruling ended *de jure segregation,* or the assigning students to schools on the basis of race rather than by neighborhood. Resistance to desegregation took many forms and ran very deep.
    B.   Civil Disobedience
- *Civil disobedience* is based on the belief that people have the right to disobey the law under certain circumstances. On December 1, 1955, Rosa Parks defied the law in Montgomery, Alabama by refusing to give up her seat on a crowed bus to a White man.
- Dr. Martin Luther King developed a strategy of nonviolent disobedience to unjust laws.
- Blacks organized a March on Washington for Jobs and Freedom on August 28, 1963. It was there that King gave his famous "I Have a Dream" speech.
    C.   Listen To Our Voices: Letter from Birmingham Jail

V.   Urban Violence and Oppression
- As violence continued during the mid-to-late 1960s, a popular explanation was that riot participants were most unemployed youths who had criminal records and who were vastly outnumbered by the African Americans who repudiated the looting and arson. This explanation was called the *riff-raff theory*.

- *Relative deprivation* is the conscious feeling of a negative discrepancy between legitimate expectations and present actualities.
- *Rising expectations* refers to the increasing sense of frustration the legitimate needs are being blocked.

VI. Black Power
- Stokely Carmichael proclaimed, "What we need is Black Power." In so doing he was distancing himself from King's goal of assimilation.
- One aspect of Black Power clearly operated out of conventional system. The Black Panther party was organized in October 1966, in Oakland, California. Huey Newton, age 24, and Bobby Seale, age 30, were the organizers and they were going to represent urban Blacks in a political climate that the Panthers felt was unresponsive.

VII. The Religious Force
- Historically, Black leaders have emerged from the pulpits to seek out rights on behalf of all Blacks.
- Despite being imposed in the past by Whites, the Christian faiths are embraced by most African Americans today. African Americans are overwhelmingly Protestant.
- A variety of non-Christian groups have exerted a much greater influence on African Americans than the reported numbers of their followers suggest. The Nation of Islam, or Black Muslims, is a case in point.

KEY TERMS

abolitionists (p. 205)	restrictive covenants (p. 211)
civil disobedience (p. 216)	riff-raff theory (p. 219)
de jure segregation (p. 214)	rising expectations (p. 219)
Ebonics (p. 204)	slave codes (p. 202)
Jim Crow (p. 206)	slavery reparations (p. 206)
relative deprivation (p. 219)	White primary (p. 206)
Sundown towns (p. 212)	Afrocentric perspective (p. 204)

PRACTICE TESTS

Practice Test One

True-False
1. T F In 1619, twenty Africans arrived in Jamestown as indentured servants.
2. T F Marriages between slaves were not legally recognized.
3. T F Reconstruction lasted from 1867 to 1877.
4. T F Abolition became law with the passage of the Civil Rights Act of 1964.
5. T F In 1935, an African American named Ruben Stacy was lynched because he had been charged with "the threatening and frightening" of a white woman.

Multiple Choice
1. Today, African Americans represent about twelve percent of the population of the United States. The projection is that by 2050, African Americans will represent approximately ____ percent of the population of the United States.
    A. fifteen
    B. twenty
    C. twenty-five
    D. thirty

2. *Jim Crow* was synonymous with _____.
    A. assimilation
    B. pluralism
    C. segregation
    D. integration

3. The *Niagara Movement*
    A. attempted to encourage Blacks to move back to the South.
    B. unmistakably placed responsibility for the problems facing African Americans on the shoulders of Whites.
    C. stressed the need for land ownership among Blacks.
    D. None of the above.

4. In 1900, _____ percent of Blacks lived in the South.
    A. 30
    B. 50
    C. 70
    D. 90

5. By 2000, _____ percent of African Americans lived in the South.
    A. 35
    B. 45
    C. 55
    D. 65

6.   The summer of _____ saw so much racial violence it became known as the "red summer."
     A. 1857
     B. 1947
     C. 1917
     D. 1964

7.   During World War II racial disturbances occurred in cities through the country. The worst riot occurred in ___ in 1943.
     A. Atlanta
     B. Baltimore
     C. Chicago
     D. Detroit

8.   It is difficult to say exactly when the Civil Rights Movement began, but our author suggests it began with
     A. the Supreme Court's decision in *Brown v. Board of Education*.
     B. Reconstruction.
     C. the Watts riots of 1965.
     D. the passage of the Civil Rights Act of 1964.

9.   On December 1, 1955, Rosa Parks defied the law and refused to give her seat on a crowded bus to a White man in _____
     A. Atlanta, Georgia.
     B. Raleigh, North Carolina.
     C. Montgomery, Alabama.
     D. Topeka, Kansas.

10. About fifty percent of African Americans identify themselves as
     A. Mormon.
     B. Catholic.
     C. Muslim.
     D. Baptist.

Short Answer Questions
1.   Identify five of the more common features of the *slave codes*.
2.   What was the *Niagara Movement*?
3.   Describe the condition of Blacks in the United States during and after World War II as presented by the author.
4.   Describe the elements of Dr. Martin Luther King's strategy of *civil disobedience*.
5.   Discuss the relationship between urban violence and oppression and the *Black Power Movement*.

Practice Test Two

True-False
1. T F For more than 100 years, the Constitution of the United States of American legally protected slavery.
2. T F Antislavery advocates were known as abolitionists.
3. T F A slave was counted as one-half of a person for determining population representation in the House of Representatives.
4. T F In 1870 there were no Blacks in the House of Representatives or in the Senate.
5. T F W.E.B. Du Bois believed that education for African Americans needed to be for vocational training rather than for academic purposes.

Multiple Choice
1. _____, along with other Blacks and sympathetic Whites, developed the Underground Railroad to convey escaping slaves to freedom in the North and Canada.
    A. W.E.B. Du Bois
    B. Harriet Tubman
    C. Booker T. Washington
    D. Fredrick Douglas

2. In 1896, the Supreme Court of the United States ruled in ____ that state laws requiring "separate but equal" accommodations for Blacks were a "reasonable" use of state government power.
    A. *Brown v. Board of Education*
    B. *Raymond v. Klein*
    C. *Plessy v. Ferguson*
    D. *Johnson v. Johnson*

3. Which of the following statements is *false*?
    A. There has not been an official government apology for slavery.
    B. The railroad industry depended heavily on slave labor for construction of railway systems.
    C. Government policy makers for the most part have not been willing to endorse the concept of slave reparations in any way.
    D. About twenty percent of Whites and forty percent of Blacks endorse some kind of cash payment to descendents of slaves.

4. Booker T. Washington's approach to White supremacy is called the politics of
    A. accommodation.
    B. hatred.
    C. revolution.
    D. civil disobedience.

5.	Which of the following was *not* a criticism raised by W.E.B. Du Bois about Booker T. Washington's perspective improving the status of Blacks?
A.	His power was used to stifle African Americans who spoke out against the politics of accommodation.
B.	He caused the transfer of funds from vocational to academic training.
C.	He encouraged Whites to place the burden of Blacks problems on Blacks themselves.
D.	Du Bois had no criticisms of Washington's perspective.

6.	The *Brown v. Board of Education* Supreme Court decision outlawed
A.	restrictive covenants.
B.	redlining.
C.	de facto segregation.
D.	de jure segregation.

7.	Dr. Martin Luther King delivered his famous "I Have a Dream" speech in
A.	Philadelphia
B.	Montgomery
C.	Washington, D.C.
D.	Memphis

8.	The popular explanation of the urban riots of the 1960s--suggesting that riot participants were mostly unemployed youths who had criminal records, often involving narcotics and who were vastly outnumbered by African Americans who repudiated the rioting and arson—was known as the _____.
A.	riff-raff theory
B.	drift hypothesis
C.	deficiency theory
D.	Davis-Moore hypothesis

9.	The Black Panther Party was organized in 1966 in _____.
A.	New York City
B.	Oakland
C.	Los Angeles
D.	Chicago

10.	He was assassinated in 1968 and is remembered most perhaps for telling Blacks to "resist violence" by any means necessary. Who was he?
A.	Booker T. Washington
B.	W.E.B. Du Bois
C.	Malcolm X
D.	Martin Luther King

Short Answer Questions

1. What were the five central conditions that *slavery* rested on?
2. What were the effects of the 1896 United States Supreme Court decision in *Plessy v. Ferguson*?
3. Differentiate between the perspectives of Booker T. Washington and W.E.B. Du Bois as Black leaders during the turn of the twentieth century.
4. Describe the demographics of African Americans in terms of religion. Briefly, what role has religion played in the social history of African Americans?
5. Identify three important points found in the civil rights movement.

ANSWERS TO PRACTICE TEST QUESTIONS

Practice Test One

True-False		Multiple Choice			
1	T (p. 201)	1.	A (p. 202)	6.	C (p. 211)
2	T (p. 202)	2.	C (p. 206)	7.	D (p. 211)
3	T (p. 205)	3.	B (p. 209)	8.	A (p. 214)
4	F (p. 205)	4.	D (p. 210)	9.	C (p. 215)
5	F (p. 211)	5.	B (p. 210)	10.	D (p. 222)

Practice Test Two

True-False		Multiple Choice			
1	T (p. 201)	1.	B (p. 205)	6.	D (p. 214)
2	T (p. 205)	2.	C (p. 206)	7.	C (p. 218)
3	F (p. 205)	3.	D (p. 207)	8.	A (p. 219)
4	F (p. 205)	4.	A (p. 208)	9.	B (p. 221)
5	F (p. 209)	5.	B (p. 209)	10.	C (p. 218)

APPLICATIONS/EXERCISES/ACTIVITIES

1. What is the relationship between Henry David Thoreau and the post-1950s civil rights movement in the United States? See the following web site for information about Thoreau:
   http://www.wsu.edu:8080/~wldciv/world_civ_reader/world_civ_reader_2/thoreau.html

2. Randomly select several high-school level American history books. Look over the section on slavery. How does it portray what type of people the slave masters were? What does it say in the discussion about the cultural backgrounds of the slaves themselves?

Chapter 7 – The Making of African Americans in a White America

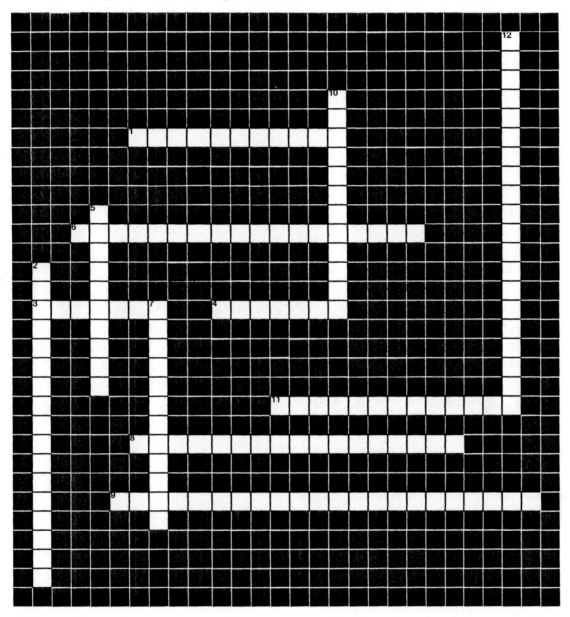

Across:

1 Relative _____ (The conscious experience of a negative discrepancy between legitimate expectations and present actualities)

3 Southern laws passed in the late 19th century that kept Blacks in their subordinate position

4 Distinctive dialect with a complex language structure found among many Black Americans

6 Acts of making amends for the injustices of slavery

8 A tactic based on the belief that people have the right to disobey unjust laws under certain circumstances

9 An emphasis on the customs of African culture and how they have pervaded the history, culture, and behavior of Black in the United States

11 Whites and free Blacks who favored the end of slavery

Down:

2 Children assigned to schools specifically to maintain racially separated schools

5 Laws that defined the low position held by slaves in the United States

7 Legal provision forbidding Black voting in election primaries, which in one-party areas of the South effectively denied Blacks their right to select elected officials

10 Communities where non-Whites were systematically excluded from living

12 Private contracts or agreements that discourage or prevent minority-group members from purchasing housing in a neighborhood

Chapter Eight

African Americans Today

CHAPTER OBJECTIVES
- To understand and evaluate the lasting impact of segregation on African American education
- To explore the assertion that some African American youth do poorly in school because they do not want to "act white."
- To learn about the general economic picture for African Americans
- To become familiar with the effects of low-income, prejudice, and discrimination on the lives of contemporary African Americans
- To explore the strengths, weaknesses, and unique challenges of African Americans families in our society
- To understand the role that housing plays in determining the quality of a person's life
- To learn about the causes and effects of residential segregation
- To become familiar with the issues African Americans face regarding the criminal justice system (including the implementation of the death penalty)
- To understand more fully the issues African Americans may face regarding issues of health care in our society
- To explore the area of politics and the issues African Americans my face in this area
- To learn about William Julius Wilson's view on what to do when work disappears

CHAPTER OUTLINE
I. Education
    A.   Quality and Quantity of Education
- Several measures document the inadequate education received by African Americans, starting with the quantity of formal education.
- A gap in the percentage of African American and White students graduating from high school still exists, though this gap is narrowing.
- Nearly twice the proportion of Whites holds a college degree as do African Americans.
- Inadequate conditions of the schools themselves are related to the higher dropout rate among African Americans.
- Although several of these problems can be addressed with more adequate funding, some are stalemated by disagreements over what changes would lead to the best outcome.

    B.   School Segregation
- Fifty years after the *Brown v. Board of Education* schools are still segregated. Now, however, it is the result of *de facto segregation*, or segregation that results from residential patterns. Seven in ten African American students attend schools in which fewer than half the students are White. Thirty-seven percent attended schools that were less than ten percent White.

- *Tracking* is a practice of placing students in specific curriculum groups on the basis of test scores and other criteria. Whites are more likely to be placed in college preparatory courses than are Blacks.
- A particularly troubling aspect of isolating Black children in schools is the apparent bias in over-identifying them as mentally retarded.

C. Acting White, Acting Black, or Neither

- A common view advances by some educators is that the reason African Americans, especially males, do not succeed in school is that they don't want to be caught "*acting White*." That is, they avoid at all costs taking school seriously and do not accept the authority of teachers and administrators.

D. Higher Education

- Although strides were made in the period after the Civil Rights movement, a plateau was reached in the mid-1970s
- African Americans are also finding the social climate on predominately White campuses less than positive. As a result, the historically Black colleges and universities are once again playing a significant role in educating African Americans.
- Several factors account for the reversal in the upward trend of African American college attendance—a reduction in financial aid, higher standards and lack of remedial programs, the need for many young Blacks to work to help financially support their families, negative publicity of affirmative action, and racial incidents on many campuses.

II. The Economic Picture

A. Income and Wealth

- *Income* refers to salaries, wages, and other money received. There is a significant gap between the incomes of Black and White families in the United States. The poverty rate for Blacks is three times that for Whites.
- *Wealth* encompasses all of a person's material assets, including land and other types of assets. The wealth picture in the United States shows even greater disparity between Whites and Blacks than does income

B. Employment

- Higher unemployment rates for Blacks have persisted since the 1940s, when they were first documented. The unemployment picture is particularly grim for African American workers aged 16 to 24
- The official unemployment rate is higher for Blacks for many reasons, including the fact that many African Americans live in the depressed economy of central cities, immigrants and illegal aliens presenting increasing competition, and more middle-class women entering the labor force.
- The official unemployment rate leaves out millions of Americans, Black and White, who are effectively unemployed. The term *underemployment* refers to working at a job for which one is overqualified, involuntarily working part-time, or being employed only intermittently.

- African Americans, who constitute twelve percent of the population, are underrepresented in high-status, high-paying occupations.
  - C. Listen to Our Voices: When Work Disappears

III. Family Life
- A. Challenges to Family Stability
  - About one-third of African American households had both a father and mother present in 2005.
  - Looming behind the issue of woman-headed families is the plight of the African American man. Simply stated, the economic status of Black men is deteriorating.
- B. Strengths of African Americans Families
  - In the midst of ever-increasing single parenting, another picture of African American family life becomes visible: success despite discrimination and economic hardship. Among the strengths of African American families include strong kinship bonds, a strong work orientation, adaptability of family roles, strong achievement orientation, and a strong religious orientation.
- C. The African American Middle Class
  - Many characteristics of African American family life have been attacked because they overemphasize the poorest segment of the African American community.
  - In 2005, nearly one-third of African Americans earned more than the median income for Whites. At least twenty-nine percent of Blacks, then, are middle class or higher.
  - African Americans are still aware of their racial subordination even when they have achieved economic equality. As many African Americans have learned, prejudice and discrimination do not end with professional status and scholarship.
  - *Class* is a term that was used by sociologist Max Weber to refer to people who share a similar level of wealth and income.
  - William J. Wilson stated that, "class has become more important than race in determining black life chances in the modern world."
  - Critics of Wilson comment that focusing attention on this small education elite ignores vast numbers of African Americans regulated to the lower-class.

IV. Housing
- The quality of Black housing is inferior to that of Whites at all income levels, yet Blacks pay a larger proportion of their income for shelter.
- Housing was the last major areas to be covered by civil rights legislation
- A. Residential Segregation
  - Among the primary factor creating residential segregation are private prejudice and discrimination, prejudicial policies of real estate companies, government policies, public housing projects, and policies of banks and other lenders.

78

- *Redlining*, relating to the last factor mentioned above, refers to the practice of discrimination against people trying to buy homes in minority and racially changing neighborhoods.
- *Zoning laws* are enacted to ensure that specific standards of housing construction will be satisfied.

V. Criminal Justice
- Data collected annually in the FBI's Uniform Crime Report show that Blacks account for twenty-eight percent of arrests, even though they represent only about thirteen percent of the population. The types of crimes included in the report and higher rates of poverty for Blacks explain these differences.
- In contrast to popular misconceptions abut crime African Americans and the poor are especially likely to be the victims of serious crimes. This fact is documented in *victimization surveys*, which are systematic interviews or ordinary people carried out annually to reveal how much crime occurs. These Department of Justice statistics show that African Americans are twenty-two percent more likely to be victims of violent crimes.
- Central to the concern that minorities often express about the criminal justice system is *differential justice*, that is, Whites are dealt with more leniently than are Blacks, whether at time of arrest, indictment, conviction, sentencing, or parole.
- *Victim discounting* refers to society's tendency to view crimes as less socially significant if the victim is viewed as less worthy.
  A.   Research Focus: The Ultimate Penalty: Execution

VI. Health Care
- Compared to Whites, Blacks have higher death rates from diseases of the heart, pneumonia, diabetes, and cancer.
- Drawing on the conflict perspective, sociologist Howard Waitzkin suggests that racial tensions contribute to the medial problems of African Americans.
- Related to the health care dilemma is the problem of environmental justice. Problems associated with toxic pollution and hazardous garbage dumps are more likely to be faced by low-income Black communities than their affluent counterparts.

VII. Politics
- After Reconstruction, it was not until 1928 that a Black was again elected to Congress. Recent years have brought some improvement in terms of the number of Black elected officials.
- *Gerrymandering* refers to the bizarre outlining of districts to create politically advantageous outcomes.
- In 2003, the Supreme Court ruled 5-4 that a state can consider over all minority influence in the political process.
- In 2006, President George W. Bush signed into law the Fannie Lou Hamer, Rosa Parks, and Coretta Scott King Voting Rights Reauthorization and Amendments Act of 2006.

KEY TERMS

class (p. 242)   tracking (p. 213)   set-asides (p. 230)

de facto segregation (p. 230) underemployment (p. 236) apartheid schools (p. 230)

differential justice (p. 245)   victim discounting (p. 246)   acting white (p. 231)

gerrymandering (p. 248)   victimization surveys (p. 245)

income (p. 234)   wealth (p. 234)

redlining (p. 244)   zoning laws (p. 244)

PRACTICE TESTS

Practice Test One

True-False

1.   T F   The proportion of Whites holding a college degree is nearly twice that of Blacks.
2.   T F   About two-thirds of Black college students attend predominately Black colleges.
3.   T F   The wealth picture in the United States shows even greater disparity between Whites and Blacks than does income.
4.   T F   Set-asides are stipulations that government contracts must be awarded in a minimum proportion, usually ten to thirty percent, to minority-owned business.
5.   T F   Between 1972 and 2001, the number of Black elected officials decreased by over ten percent.

Multiple Choice

1.   In 2004, 32.9 percent of Whites males over the age of twenty-five years of age had a college degree. What was the corresponding percentage for Black males?
   A. 2.8
   B. 7.2
   C. 21.7
   D. 28.4

2.   School segregation resulting from residential patterns refers to _____ segregation.
   A. de jure
   B. de facto
   C. residual
   D. tracking

3. In 2005, about eight percent of non-Hispanic Whites lived below the poverty line in the United States. What was the corresponding figure for Blacks?
   A. 12
   B. 17
   C. 24
   D. 35

4. Since 1990, the *national unemployment rate* for Whites has ranged from 3 to 6 percent. The corresponding figures for Black are from _____ percent.
   A. 7-11
   B. 12-18
   C. 21-29
   D. 35-46

5. In 2004, African Americans accounted for what percentage of *professional and managerial occupations*?
   A. 2
   B. 5
   C. 6
   D. 10

6. Legal provisions stipulating land use and the architectural design of housing, often used to keep racial minorities and low-income people out of suburban areas is/are called:
   A. zoning laws.
   B. redlining.
   C. blue lining.
   D. city laws.

7. Victim discounting is a major factor in
   A. White on White crime.
   B. White on Black crime.
   C. Black on White crime.
   D. Black on Black crime.

8. William Julius Wilson has found young Black males
   A. embraced the culture of poverty.
   B. compete successfully with young Whites.
   C. reject family ties.
   D. prefer all-Black universities.

9. The practice of discriminating against people trying to buy homes in minority and racially changing neighborhoods refers to
   A. differential justice.
   B. gerrymandering.
   C. redlining.
   D. tracking.

10. Whites being dealt with more leniently than are Blacks, whether at the time of arrest, indictment, conviction, sentencing, or parole is known as
   A. differential justice.
   B. redlining.
   C. tracking.
   D. victim discounting.

Short Answer Questions
1. Although African Americans are more likely today to be college graduates, the upward trend has declined. What factors are identified in the text for this reversal?
2. The future of Black-owned businesses is uncertain. What are three factors that are creating obstacles for Black-owned businesses?
3. How does the African American family and White family compare demographically?
4. In what ways has *gerrymandering* both helped and hindered Blacks politically in the United States?
5. What are three conclusions drawn by the author of the text concerning Blacks in the United States?

Practice Test Two

True-False
1. T F William J. Wilson wrote the *Declining Significance of Race*.
2. T F In terms of *absolute deprivation*, African Americans are much better off today than forty years ago but have experienced much less significant improvement with respect to their *relative deprivation*.
3. T F Black men typically earn less than their White male colleagues in similar positions.
4. T F Tracking is the practice of placing students in specific curriculum groups on the basis of test scores and other criteria.
5. T F *Housing* was the last major area covered by civil rights legislation.

Multiple Choice
1. *Gerrymandering* is a concept relating to
   A. criminal justice.
   B. politics.
   C. education.
   D. income.

2. Which of the following is typical of African American families?
   A. low achievement orientation
   B. low achievement aspirations
   C. a strong work orientation
   D. rigid family roles

3. The most consistently documented strength of the Black family is the presence of:
   A. a strong male wage earner.
   B. a public childcare for working mothers.
   C. an extended family household.
   D. the Black church.

4. _____ *employment* refers to working at job for which one is overqualified, involuntarily working part-time, or being employed only intermittently.
   A. Residual
   B. Under
   C. Real
   D. Actual

5. In 2002, most African American workers were in which of the following professional occupations?
   A. teachers
   B. social workers
   C. lawyers
   D. registered nurses

6. What percentage of Black families are two-parent families?
   A. 15
   B. 25
   C. 50
   D. 65

7. The complexity of the relative influence of race and _____ was apparent in the controversy surrounding the publication of sociologist William Julius Wilson's *The Declining Significance of Race*.
   A. age
   B. gender
   C. family
   D. class

8. The FBI's Uniform Crime Report (UCR) focuses on:
   A. property crimes.
   B. index crimes.
   C. violent crime.
   D. crimes against people.

9. White male Americans can expect to live 75.0 years. By contrast, *life expectancy* for African Americans males is
   A. 57.4.
   B. 72.4.
   C. 61.9.
   D. 68.6.

10. A bizarre outlining of districts to create politically advantageous outcomes refers to
    A. gerrymandering.
    B. reappropriation.
    C. de facto segregation.
    D. redlining.

Short Answer Questions
1. What educational inadequacies are identified in the text that increase the *dropout rate* of African American students?
2. What factors are involved in explaining why *unemployment rates* for young African Americans are so high?
3. In what ways is *tracking* a part of school segregation in the United States?
4. What are five strengths of African American families today?
5. What is the evidence presented in the text concerning racial inequality in our *criminal justice system*?

ANSWERS TO PRACTICE TEST QUESTIONS

Practice Test One

True-False		Multiple Choice			
1.	T (p. 229)	1.	C (p. 229)	6.	A (p. 249)
2.	F (p. 233)	2.	B (p. 230)	7.	D (p. 246)
3.	T (p. 235)	3.	C (p. 235)	8.	B (p. 237)
4.	T (p. 236)	4.	A (p. 236)	9.	C (p. 244)
5.	F (p. 248)	5.	B (p. 235)	10.	A (p. 245)

Practice Test Two

True-False		Multiple Choice			
1.	T (p. 242)	1.	B (p. 248)	6.	C (p. 239)
2.	T (p. 234)	2.	C (p. 240)	7.	D (p. 242)
3.	T (p. 238)	3.	C (p. 241)	8.	B (p. 245)
4.	T (p. 230)	4.	B (p. 236)	9.	D (p. 246)
5.	T (p. 243)	5.	B (p. 238)	10.	A (p. 248)

APPLICATIONS/EXERCISES/ACTIVITIES

1. Visit the web site for The Black World Today (http://www.tbwt.org/)
    and find a topic that you can analyze using functionalist and conflict theories.
    Explain the theories in detail and use them to analyze the topic that you have
    selected.

2. Write down the name of ten famous African Americans. Compare your results
    with the comparable national data for 17 year olds and adults in the publication by
    the U.S. Government Printing Office, 2004, "Contemporary Social Issues,
    National Assessment of Education Progress.

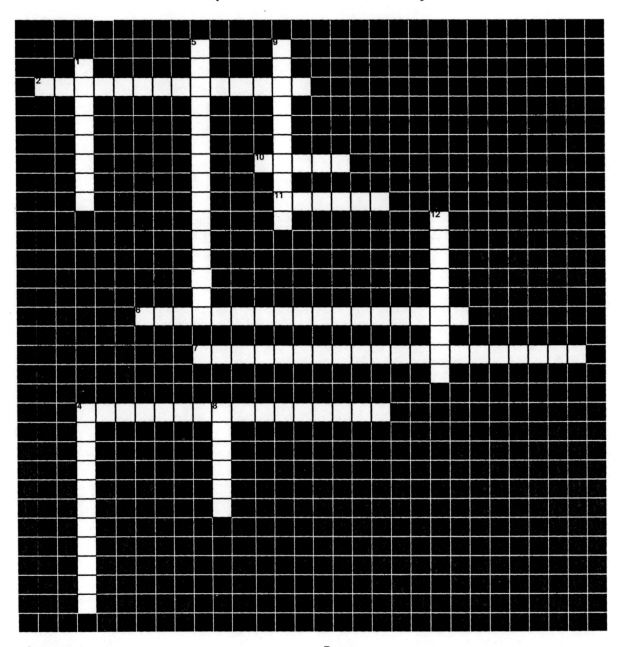

Across:

2 Redrawing districts bizarrely to create politically advantageous outcomes

4 All-Black schools

6 Tendency to view crime as less socially significant if the victim is viewed as less worthy

7 Annual attempts to measure crime rates by interviewing ordinary citizens who may or may not have been crime victims

10 People who share similar levels of wealth

11 An inclusive term encompassing all of a person's material assets, including land and other types of property

Down:

1 The practice of placing students in specific curriculum groups on the basis of test scores and other criteria

4 Taking school seriously and accepting the authority of teachers and administrators

5 Work at a job for which the worker is overqualified, involuntary part-time instead of full-time employment, or intermittent employment

8 Salaries, wages, and other money received

9 Legal provisions stipulating land use and the architectural design of housing, often used to keep racial minorities and low-income people out of suburban areas

12 The pattern of discrimination against people trying to buy homes in minority and racially changing neighborhoods

Chapter Nine

Hispanic Americans

CHAPTER OBJECTIVES
- To learn about the diversity of the Latino American or Hispanic population in the United States
- To understand and explore the different ideas that encompass the concept "Latino Identity"
- To evaluate the role of panethnicity in the Hispanic community
- To understand the overall economic picture of Latinos as a groups
- To learn about and understand the importance of the Quinceanera
- To understand and evaluate the growing political presence of Latino political involvement in the United States
- To understand the significance of the borderlands to Mexicans and Mexican Americans as well as other Hispanic groups
- To understand the experiences of Cuban immigrants in the United States and the issues they face as they remain in this country
- To understand the diversity of immigrants who have come from Central and South America
- To understand and evaluate the importance of the color gradient in the social construction of race

CHAPTER OUTLINE
I.   Latino Identity
- More than one in eight people in the United States today are of Spanish or Latin American origin. The Census Bureau estimates this figure will reach one in three by the year 2100.
- Latino or Hispanic influence is found throughout the United States. Today, ninety-one percent of Latinos/Hispanics live in metropolitan areas.
- Only a minority, one in four Hispanics/Latinos prefers to use pan-ethnic terms such as Hispanic or Latino. The majority of Hispanics prefer identifying themselves by nationality.
   A.   Research Focus: Latinos: American Style

II. The Economic Picture
- The median household income of Latinos has increased over the last twenty years.
- Latino households can expect to earn 70 cents on the dollar received by its White counterpart.
- The proportion of Latinos in poverty has been two or three times that of non-Hispanic Whites.

III. The Growing Political Presence
- Federal law now requires bilingual or even multilingual ballets in voting districts where at least five percent of the population belongs to a single minority group. The potential for a greater Latino political presence is strong.
- The major political parties are more likely to see that the Latino vote is still in play.

IV. The Borderlands
- The term "borderlands" refers to the area of a common culture along the border between Mexico and the United States.
- Very visible is the presence of *maquiladoras,* or foreign-owned companies that establish operations in Mexico yet are exempt from Mexican taxes and are not required to provide insurance or benefits for their workers.
- Many Mexicans, as well as other Hispanic groups, send some part of their earnings back across the border to family members remaining in their native country. This flow of money is sometimes called remittances (or migradollars).
- Hometown clubs typically are nonprofit organizations that maintain close ties to immigrants' hometowns in Mexico and other Latin American countries.

V. Cuban Americans
A. Immigration
- Cuban immigration to the United States since the 1959 revolution has been continuous, but there have been three significant influxes of large numbers of immigrants through the 1980s.
- Some Cubans began to call the refugees of the third wave of migration *Marielitos.*
- The Cuban refuge situation continues to be caught up in the strong anti-Castro, anticommunist feelings of most Cuban Americans and many others in the United States.
B. Listen to Our Voices: Leaving Cuba
C. The Present Picture
- Compared with other recent immigrant groups and with Latinos as a whole, Cuban Americans are doing well.
- Most Cuban Americans live in the Miami area.
- The primary adjustment among south Florida's Cuban Americans is more to each other than to Whites, African Americans, or other Latinos.
- The long-range prospects for Cubans in the United States depend on several factors.
- Cubans have selectively accepted Anglo culture.

VI. Central and South Americans
- The immigrants who have come from Central and South America are a diverse population that has not been closely studied.
- Many of the nations in Central and South America have a complex system of

placing people into myriad racial groups. A *color gradient* is the placement of people along a continuum from light to dark skin color than in distinct racial groupings by skin color.
- There are social class differences, religion differences, urban-versus-rural backgrounds, and differences in dialect even among those speaking the same language.

A. Immigration
- Immigration from the various Central and South American nations has been sporadic, influenced by both our immigration laws and social forces operating in the home country

B. The Present Picture
- The recent settlement of Central and South Americans has been clouded by two issues. First, many of the arrivals are illegal immigrants. Second, significant numbers of highly trained and skilled people have left these countries which are in great need of professional workers—the *brain drain* problem.

KEY TERMS

dry foot, wet foot (p. 266)   ethclass (p. 257)

Quinceanera (p. 258)   hometown clubs (p. 263)

borderlands (p. 262)   maquiladoras (p. 263)

brain drain (p. 269)   Marielitos (p. 264)

color gradient (p. 268)   panethnicity (p. 255)

remittances (or migradollars) (p. 263)

PRACTICE TESTS

Practice Test One

True-False
1.   T F   The largest percentage of Hispanic Americans is Puerto Ricans.
2.   T F   Most Hispanic Americans prefer to identify themselves by nationality.
3.   T F   Mexican Americans and the Puerto Ricans are by far the two largest Latino groups in the U.S.
4.   T F   *Remittances* is a term referring to taxes paid by Mexico to the United States for United States workers who cross the border to work in Mexican companies.
5.   T F   Compared with other recent immigrant groups and with Latinos as a whole, Cuban Americans are doing well.

Multiple Choice

1. More than one in _____ people in the United States are of Spanish or Latin American origin.
   A. 3
   B. 8
   C. 12
   D. 16

2. The celebration of Latinas turning 15 years of age is
   A. Quinceanera
   B. Vientera
   C. Mientera
   D. a birthday party

3. _____ refers to the development of solidarity between ethnic subgroups.
   A. Functionalism
   B. Labeling
   C. Xenophobia
   D. Panethnicity

4. _____ refers to the area of common culture along the border between Mexico and the United States.
   A. Panterma
   B. Pan-lands
   C. Terra gradient
   D. Borderlands

5. *Maquiladoras* are
   A. foreign-owned companies that establish operations in Mexico yet are exempt from Mexican taxes and are not required to provide insurance or benefits for their workers.
   B. schools in areas near the border of Mexico and the United States that structure bilingualism into their educational curricula.
   C. workers who are citizens of the United States but who work for companies in Mexico where jobs are more plentiful.
   D. None of the above.

6. Many Hispanic Americans send some part of their earnings back across the border to family members remaining in their native country. This substantial flow of money is referred to as
   A. Marielitos.
   B. remittances.
   C. maquiladoras.
   D. hometown clubs.

7. Republicans favor
   A. reducing legal immigration.
   B. limiting welfare benefits to legal immigrants.
   C. eliminating bilingual education.
   D. all of the above.

8. The largest Hispanic group in the U.S. after Chicanos and Puerto Ricans is:
   A. Salvadorans.
   B. Brazilians.
   C. Cubans.
   D. Haitians.

9. Terms such as *mestizo, Hondurans, mulatto, Columbians,* and *African Panamanians* reflect which concept?
   A. panethnicity
   B. remittances
   C. immersion
   D. color gradient

10. The U.S. has a "dry foot, wet foot" policy with respect to arrivals from
    A. Cuba.
    B. Mexico.
    C. Puerto Rico.
    D. Haiti.

Short Answer Questions
1. What is the evidence that Hispanics or Latinos are developing a common identity?
2. What is meant by the term "panethnicity?"
3. Describe the relative status of Cuban Americans compared to other Hispanic groups in the United States?
4. What is meant by the term *color gradient*? What are the pros and cons of such an understanding of racial groupings?
5. Describe Hispanic Americans as a political force in our society.

Practice Test Two

True-False
1. T F Hispanics and Latino Americans share a common linguistic heritage.
2. T F Already by 2005, population data showed 41.9 million Latinos outnumbering the 39 million African Americans.
3. T F Cuban Americans have selectively accepted Anglo culture.
4. T F The population of metropolitan Miami is over one-third *foreign-born.*
5. T F The immigrants who come from Central and South America represent a relatively homogeneous group.

Multiple Choice

1. _____ is the development of solidarity between ethnic subgroups.
   A. Ethclass
   B. Pluralism
   C. Panethnicity
   D. Ethnocentrism

2. Which of the following terms is the most widely used in the West?
   A. Hispanic
   B. Latino
   C. Latin American
   D. Spanish American

3. In 2000, Elian Gonzalez
   A. was returned to Cuba with his father.
   B. was allowed to remain in the U.S. with his father.
   C. was returned to Cuba without his father.
   D. was allowed to remain in the U.S. but without his father.

4. The nation's largest Spanish-language newspaper is called
   A. Notimex.
   B. La Opinion.
   C. El Derecho.
   D. Las Noticias.

5. In 1997, _____ was criticized for the content of its manual for pilots flying between the U.S. and Latin America.
   A. United Airlines
   B. Northwest Airlines
   C. American Airlines
   D. Continental Airlines

6. _____ are typically non-profit organizations that maintain close ties to immigrants' hometowns in Mexico and other Latin American countries.
   A. Marielitos
   B. Hometown clubs
   C. Migratowns
   D. Border organizations

7. An agreement between the United States and ____ in 1965 produced a number of immigrants through a program called "Freedom Flight."
   A. Haiti
   B. the Dominican Republic
   C. Cuba
   D. Columbia

8.   Cubans call some refugees of the migration from Castro's Cuba who have arrived
      since 1980
      A. regaletos.
      B. maquiladoras.
      C. remittances.
      D. Marielitos.

9.   The color gradient is Central and South America refers to
      A. skin color.
      B. language and literacy.
      C. class.
      D. education.

10.   Among the factors that distinguish Central and South Americans in the U.S. from
      each other is
      A. language.
      B. skin color.
      C. social class.
      D. all of the above.

Short Answer Questions
1.   What is meant by the view that Hispanics are an *invisible minority*?
2.   Differentiate between the arguments being made by proponents of *English
      immersion* and proponents of *bilingual education*.
3.   How is immigration from South America and Central America countries other
      than Mexico different from immigration from Mexico?
4.   What are the relative advantages and disadvantages for Mexico and the United
      States concerning *maquiladora*?
5.   What are the general conclusions being made by the author concerning Hispanic
      Americas' relative position in society?

ANSWERS TO PRACTICE TEST QUESTIONS

Practice Test One

True-False		Multiple Choice			
1.	F (p. 254)	1.	B (p. 254)	6.	B (p. 263)
2.	T (p. 256)	2.	A (p. 258)	7.	A (p. 261)
3.	T (p. 264)	3.	D (p. 255)	8.	C (p. 264)
4.	F (p. 263)	4.	D (p. 262)	9.	D (p. 268)
5.	T (p. 266)	5.	A (p. 263)	10.	A (p. 266)

Practice Test Two

True-False		**Multiple Choice**			
1.	T (p. 253)	1.	C (p. 255)	6.	B (p. 263)
2.	T (p. 254)	2.	B (p. 256)	7.	C (p. 264)
3.	T (p. 267)	3.	A (p. 266)	8.	D (p. 264)
4.	T (p. 267)	4.	C (p. 236)	9.	A (p. 268)
5.	F (p. 268)	5.	C (p. 254)	10.	D (p. 268)

APPLICATIONS/EXERCISES/ACTIVITIES

1. Analyze the attacks on bilingual education from both a functionalist and a conflict perspective by using data from The Office of Bilingual Education and Minority Language Affairs (http://www.ed.gov/about/offices/list/oela/index.html?src=mr) to support your argument.

2. The on-line publication Hispanic Magazine.com features news on Latino and Hispanic Americans in the areas of culture, business, education, politics and other interesting topics. Their website is: http://www.hispaniconline.com/magazine/

Chapter 9 – Hispanic Americans

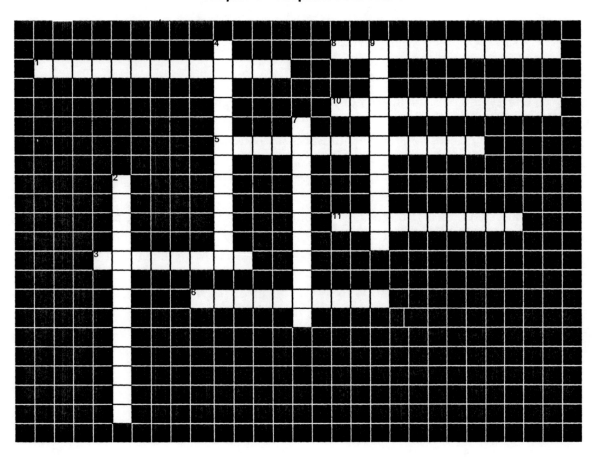

Across:

1 The placement of people on a continuum from light to dark skin color rather than in distinct racial groupings by skin color

3 The merged ethnicity and class in a person's status

5 Policy toward Cuban immigrants allowing entry to those who manage to reach the US to remain, while those picked-up at sea are sent back to Cuba

6 Immigration to the United States of skilled workers, professionals, and technicians who are desperately needed by their home countries

8 Foreign-owned companies on the Mexican side of the border with the United States

10 The development of solidarity between ethnic subgroups, as reflected in the terms *Hispanic* or *Asian American*

11 People who arrived from Cuba in the third wave of Cuban immigration, most specifically those forcibly deported by way of Mariel Harbor. The term is generally reserved for refugees seen as especially undesirable

Down:

2 Nonprofit organizations that maintain close ties to immigrants' hometowns in Mexico and other Latin American countries

4 (or remittances) The money that immigrant workers send back to families in their native societies

7 The area of a common culture along the border between Mexico and the United States

9 Celebration of Latinas turning 15 years of age

Chapter Ten

Mexican Americans and Puerto Ricans

CHAPTER OBJECTIVES
- To understand how the history of Mexican Americans is closely tied to immigration
- To explore the economic picture of Mexican Americans
- To understand and evaluate the culture of poverty
- To understand the role that Cesar Chavez and the United Farm Workers in the changing of Mexican Americans lives
- To understand the role of political organizations and contemporary political issues in the lives of Mexican Americans
- To understand how Puerto Ricans' current association with the United States began as the result of the outcome of a war
- To explore the unique situation that Puerto Ricans have concerning the bridge between the Island of Puerto Rico and the mainland
- To become familiar with the issues of statehood and self-rule for Puerto Rico
- To understand the differences in the meaning of race in Puerto Rico and on the mainland
- To explore the economic picture of Puerto Ricans
- To be introduced to the situation of Mexican Americans and Puerto Ricans in the United States in regard to education, family life, health care and religion.

CHAPTER OUTLINE
I. Mexican Americans
   - In 1821, Mexico obtained its independence, but its independence was short-lived, for domination from the north began less than a generation later.
   - A large number of Mexicans became aliens in the United States without ever crossing any border. These people first became Mexican Americans with the conclusion of the Mexican—American War. In the Treaty of Guadalupe Hidalgo, signed in 1848, Mexico acknowledged the annexation of Texas by the United States and ceded California, and most of Arizona and New Mexico to the United States for $15 million.
   - One generalization can be made about the many segments of the Mexican American population in the nineteenth century: they were regarded as a conquered people.
   A. The Immigrant Experience
      - The United States did not restrict immigration from Mexico through legislation until 1965.
      - Immigration from Mexico is unique in several respects. First, there has been continuous large-scale movement for most of the twentieth century. Second, the close proximity of Mexico encourages past immigrants to maintain close cultural and language ties with the

homeland through friends and relatives. Third, there is the aura of illegal immigrants that has surrounded Mexican immigrants.

- The Mexican revolution of 1909-1922 thrust refugees into the United States, and World War I curtailed the flow of people from Europe, leaving the labor market open to the Mexican Americans.
- The period of deporting Mexicans in the 1930s was called *repatriation*.
- The *bracero* program, beginning in 1942, brought Mexican nationals into the United States as contracted workers.
- *Mojados*, or wetbacks, is the slang for Mexicans who enter illegally, supposedly by swimming the Rio Grande.
- Assimilation may be the key word in the history of many immigrant groups, but for Mexican Americans the key term is *La Raza*, literally meaning "the people."

B. The Economic Picture
- The *culture of poverty* embraces a deviant way of life that involves no future orient planning, no enduring commitment to marriage, and absence of the work ethic. This view is another way of blaming the victim.
- Research shows that when Anglo and Mexican American families of the same social class are compared, they differ little in family organization and attitudes toward childrearing.
- The best-known Hispanic labor leader for economic empowerment was Cesar Chavez, the Mexican American who crusaded to organize migrant farm workers. He formed the United Farm Workers in 1962.

C. Political Organizations
- In Southern California in 1966, young Chicanos in college were attracted to the ideology of *Chicanismo* and joined what is called the Chicano movement. Like Black Power, Chicanismo has taken on a variety of meanings, but all definitions stress a positive self-image and place little reliance on conventional forms of political activity.
- Beginning in 1998, Mexicans in the United States could acquire rights as Mexican nationals under Mexico's new dual nationality law.
- In 1997, the goals of Tijerina and his followers are finally being considered seriously.

II. Puerto Ricans
- The United States seized Puerto Rico in 1898 during the Spanish-American War. Citizenship was extended to Puerto Ricans by the Jones Act of 1917, but Puerto Rico remained a colony.
- In 1948, Puerto Rico elected its own Governor and became a common wealth.

A. The Bridge Between the Island and the Mainland
- The major migration of Puerto Ricans to the United States has been largely a post-World War II phenomenon.
- *Neoricans* are Puerto Ricans returning to the island after having spent time in the United States.

- Over the last ten years, Mexican and Mexican arrivals in New York City have far outpaced any growth among Puerto Ricans.
   B. The Island of Puerto Rico
- Puerto Rico and its people reflect a phenomenon called *neocolonialism, which refers to continuing dependence of former colonies on foreign countries.*
- Issues of Statehood and self-rule.
- Puerto Ricans have periodically argued and fought for independence for most of the 500 years since Columbus landed.
- Puerto Rico's future status most recently faced a vote in 1998. In the latest nonbonding referendum, fifty percent favored continuing commonwealth status, and forty-seven percent favored statehood. Less than three percent favored independence.
- The social construction of race.
- Puerto Rican migrants to the mainland must make adjustments in language, housing, and employment.
- The most significant difference between the meaning of race on Puerto Rico and the mainland is that Puerto Rico, like so many other Caribbean societies, has a color gradient. The term *color gradient* describes distinctions based on skin color made on a continuum rather than by sharp categorical separations.
- Racial identity in Puerto Rico depends a great deal on the attitude of the individual making the judgment.
   C. Listen to Our Voices: Viva Vieques!
   D. The Island Economy
- The United States' role in Puerto Rico has produced an overall economy that, though strong by Caribbean standards, remains well below that of the poorest areas of the United States. Puerto Rico's unemployment rate is three times that of the mainland.
- *World systems theory* is the view of the global economic system as divided between certain industrialized nations that control wealth and developing countries that are controlled and exploited.
- Another major factor in the economy is tourism.
- The North American Trade Agreement confronts Puerto Rico with new challenges.

III. The Contemporary Picture of Mexican Americans and Puerto Ricans
   A. Education
- Latinos, including Mexican Americans and Puerto Ricans have become increasingly segregated.
- *Tracking* is also an issue.
   B. Family Life
- *Familism* means pride and closeness in the family, which results in family obligation and loyalty coming before individual needs.

- *Compadrazgo*, the God Parent-God Child relationship, is an important aspect of familism.
C. Health Care
   - Latinos consistently have more limited *life chances*, or opportunities to provide themselves with material goods, positive living conditions, and favorable life experiences than do Whites.
   - A third of Hispanics have no health insurance. The health care problem facing Mexican Americans and other Hispanic groups is complicated by the lack of Hispanic health professionals.
   - Some Mexican Americans and many other Latinos have cultural beliefs that make them less likely to use the medical system. They may interpret their illnesses according to folk practices or *curanderismo*.
D. Research Focus: Assimilation May Be Hazardous to Your Health
E. Religion
   - The most important formal organization in the Hispanic community is the church. Most Puerto Ricans and Mexican Americans express a religious preference for the Catholic Church, which has played an assimilationist role.
   - Although Latinos are predominately Catholic, their membership in Protestant and other Christian faiths is growing.
   - *Pentecostalism*, a type of evangelical Christianity, is growing in Latin America and is clearly making a significant impact on Latinos in the United States.

KEY TERMS

bracero (p. 276)	*mojados* (p. 277)
Chicanismo (p. 281)	neocolonialism (p. 285)
color gradient (p. 289)	Neoricans (p. 284)
culture of poverty (p. 289)	Pentecostalism (p. 295)
curanderismo (p. 278)	repatriation (p. 276)
familism (p. 292)	tracking (p. 291)
La Raza (p. 277)	world systems theory (p. 290)
life chances (p. 292)	

PRACTICE TESTS

Practice Test One

True-False

1.   T F   The United States did not restrict immigration from Mexico through legislation until 1965.
2.   T F   The *culture-of-poverty* view puts the blame for economic inequality between Whites and minority groups on the dominant society.
3.   T F   The *color gradient* is a term used to describe the changing ethnic characteristics of urban neighborhoods.
4.   T F   The Roman Catholic Church took a *pluralistic* orientated role in the past, whether with Hispanic Catholics or with other minority Catholics.
5.   T F   Although Latinos are predominately Catholic, their membership in Protestant and other Christian faiths is growing.

Multiple Choice

1.   In _____ Mexico obtained its independence.
   A. 1596
   B. 1838
   C. 1821
   D. 1902

2.   The United States began to restrict immigration from Mexico through legislation in
   A. 1789.
   B. 1838.
   C. 1930s.
   D. 1965.

3.   The program of deporting Mexicans in the 1930s was called
   A. repatriation.
   B. bracero.
   C. La Raza.
   D. mojados

4.   The best-known Hispanic labor leader for economic empowerment was Cesar Chavez, the Mexican American who crusaded to organize _____ workers.
   A. construction
   B. hotel
   C. migrant farm
   D. factory

5.   The United States seized Puerto Rico during the Spanish-American War in
       A. 1812.
       B. 1898.
       C. 1848.
       D. 1912.

6.   Citizenship was extended to Puerto Ricans in _____.
       A. 1848
       B. 1898
       C. 1917
       D. 1953

7.   Puerto Ricans returning to the Island of Puerto Rico after living in the United
       States have come to be known as
       A. Neoricans.
       B. mojados.
       C. repatriots.
       D. braceros.

8.   The Treaty of Guadalupe Hidalgo represents
       A. expulsion.
       B. segregation.
       C. pluralism.
       D. secession.

9.   The world systems theory views developing countries as
       A. controlled and exploited.
       B. independent and resilient.
       C. powerful and resourceful.
       D. traditional and ethnocentric.

10.   *Curanderismo* means
       A. the people.
       B. folk medicine.
       C. self-esteem.
       D. exploitation.

Short-Answer Questions
1.   What factors make immigration from Mexico unique?
2.   What was the *bracero program*?
3.   Describe Cesar Chavez's role as a labor leader among Mexican Americans.
4.   What are the pros and cons for Puerto Ricans in terms of gaining U.S. statehood?
5.   Describe the demographic patterns found among Mexican Americans and Puerto
       Ricans in terms of religious affiliation.

Practice Test Two

True-False

1.   T F   World War I significantly curtailed immigration from Mexico.
2.   T F   Puerto Ricans have the highest median family income of all Hispanic groups in the United States.
3.   T F   Citizenship was extended to Puerto Ricans by the Jones Act of 1917.
4.   T F   Puerto Rico and its people reflect a phenomenon called *neocolonialism*.
5.   T F   Most Latinos in the U.S. live in New York City.

Multiple Choice

1. The Mexican-American War ended in
   A. 1783.
   B. 1848.
   C. 1895.
   D. 1922.

2. The *bracero program*
   A. allowed for migration across the Mexican-U.S. border by contracted workers.
   B. provided reparations for lands taken during the Mexican-American War.
   C. created English as a second language in borderland areas.
   D. established deportation requirements for illegal aliens.

3. *La Raza* means
   A. the land.
   B. the way.
   C. the people
   D. the workers

4. Puerto Rico is located
   A. east of the Dominican Republic.
   B. south of Jamaica.
   C. southwest of Cuba.
   D. north of Haiti.

5. In 2005, Puerto Rico had a population of about 3.9 million. The population of Puerto Ricans in the
   United States is _____ million.
   A. 1.2
   B. 2.2
   C. 3.8
   D. 5.9

6. Bilingual education best represents which of the following?
   A. secession
   B. assimilation
   C. pluralism
   D. segregation

7. The continuing dependence of former colonies on foreign countries refers to
   A. fusion.
   B. assimilation.
   C. secession.
   D. neocolonialism.

8. Recent polls in Puerto Rico indicate that _____ percent of the Islanders favor independence from the United States.
   A. 3
   B. 25
   C. 50
   D. 65

9. In 1968 about fifty-five percent of all Hispanics attended predominantly minority schools, that is, schools in which at least half of the students were members of minorities. Today, this rate is about _____ percent.
   A. 11
   B. 27
   C. 52
   D. 76

10. Which of the following U.S. cities has the second largest number of Latinos?
    A. New York City
    B. Los Angeles
    C. Miami
    D. Houston

Short-Answer Questions
1. Describe the history of the relationships between the United States and Puerto Rico as presented in the text.
2. In what ways do Puerto Rico and its people reflect the phenomenon of *neocolonialism*?
3. In what way is Puerto Rico an example of *world systems theory*?
4. Describe the relative status of Mexican Americans and Puerto Ricans in terms of education. What three factors are creating greater segregation for Latino students?
5. Describe the role played by the practices of *curanderismo* for Mexican American health care.

ANSWERS TO PRACTICE TEST QUESTIONS

Practice Test One

True-False		Multiple Choice			
1.	T (p. 274)	1.	C (p. 275)	6.	C (p. 283)
2.	T (p. 278)	2.	C (p. 276)	7.	A (p. 284)
3.	F (p. 289)	3.	A (p. 276)	8.	D (p. 284)
4.	F (p. 294)	4.	C (p. 279)	9.	A (p. 290)
5.	T (p. 295)	5.	B (p. 282)	10.	B (p. 294)

Practice Test Two

True-False		Multiple Choice			
1.	F (p. 276)	1.	B (p. 275)	6.	C (p. 284)
2.	F (p. 278)	2.	A (p. 276)	7.	D (p. 285)
3.	T (p. 283)	3.	C (p. 277)	8.	A (p. 288)
4.	T (p. 285)	4.	A (p. 282)	9.	D (p. 290)
5.	T (p. 296)	5.	C (p. 283)	10.	B (p. 296)

APPLICATIONS/EXERCISES/ACTIVITIES

1. Go to the following two web sites:
   http://www.aclu-or.org/legislature/national/immigrants1.htm and
   http://www.fas.org/irp/world/para/faln.htm and use either the functionalist
   perspective or conflict theory to analyze the similarities or differences between
   the movements that are discussed at each site.

2. Critically listen to the song "America" from the musical "West Side Story."
   Listen to the words. What does the song say and not say about the relative merits
   of life in New York City as compared to life on the island of Puerto Rico?

Chapter 10 – Mexican Americans and Puerto Ricans

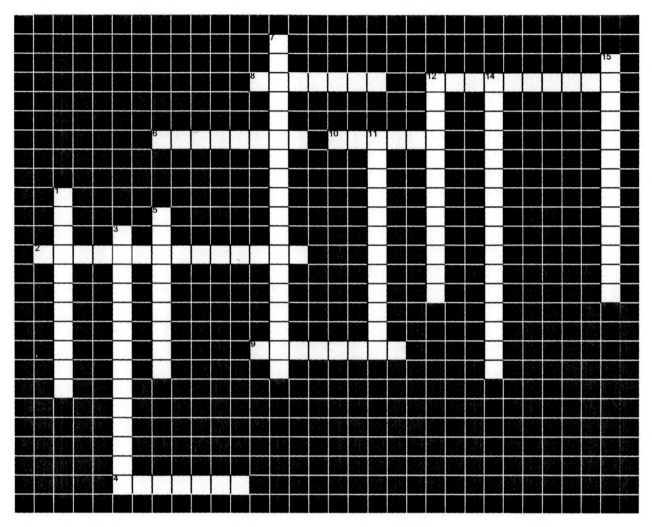

Across:

2 A religion that believes in the infusion of the Holy Spirit into services and in religious experiences such as faith healing

4 "Wetbacks" Derisive slang for Mexicans who enter illegally, supposedly by swimming the Rio Grande

6 Pride of closeness in the family that result in placing family obligation and loyalty before individual needs

8 Contracted Mexican laborers brought to the United States during World War II

9 The practice of placing students in specific curriculum groups on the basis of test scores and other criteria

10 "The People" a term referring to the rich heritage of Mexican Americans and therefore used to denote a sense of pride among Mexican Americans today

12 An ideology emphasizing pride and positive identity among Mexican Americans

Down:

1 People's opportunities to provide themselves with material goods, positive living conditions, and favorable life experiences

3 Continuing dependence of former colonies on foreign countries

5 Puerto Ricans who return to the island to settle after living on the mainland of the United States

7 The global economic system is divided between nations and control wealth and those that provide natural resources and labor

11 The 1930s program deporting Mexicans

12 Hispanic folk medicine

14 A way of life that involves no future planning, no enduring commitment to marriage, and no work ethic; this culture follows the poor even when they move out of the slums to the barrio

15 The placement of people on a continuum from light to dark skin rather than in distinct racial groupings by skin color

Chapter Eleven

Muslim and Arab Americans: Diverse Minorities

CHAPTER OBJECTIVES
- To understand that Muslim and Arab Americans are different groups in the United States
- To evaluate the deficit model of ethnic behavior as it applies to Arab Americans
- To understand Arab Americans and the characteristics of the Arab American community
- To understand Muslim Americans and the characteristics of Muslim American communities
- To evaluate the blended identity self-image and worldview and how it applies to Muslim Americans
- To learn about Black Muslims and their history in the United States
- To learn about the experiences of Muslim and Arab American immigrants to the United States
- To understand contemporary life in the United States for Muslim and Arab Americans
- To learn how life might have changed for Muslim and Arab Americans since 9/11
- To examine what it means to be Arab or Muslim in the United States today
- To gain awareness of current issues of prejudice and discrimination toward Arab and Muslim Americans

CHAPTER OUTLINE
I. Muslim and Arab People
- The Arab and Muslim American communities are among the most rapidly growing subordinate groups in the U.S.
- Arabs are an ethnic group. Muslims are a religious group. Islam is the faith (like Christianity). A Muslim is a believer of that religion (like a Christian)

II. Arab Americans
- The Arabic language is the single most unifying force among Arabs. Two-thirds of Arab Americans in 2000 came from Lebanon, Syria, Egypt, and Palestine.
- Diversity underlies virtually everything about Arab Americans in three distinct ways, time of arrival, the point of origin, and a rich variety of religious tradition.
- The *deficit model of ethnic identity* is important in studying Arab Americans.

III. Muslim Americans
- Islam is guided by the teachings of Qur'an, the collected sayings or *hadeeth*, and deeds of the seventh century Prophet Mohammad. Governments in Muslim countries often reinforce Islamic practices through their laws.

Muslims participate in religious rituals and are divided into a variety of faiths and sects.

- Muslim Americans reflect a *blended identity*.
- What makes the American Muslim experience unique is that followers must place even stronger focus on Islam in order to survive in a culture that is so permissive, and indeed, encourages behavior that is prohibited by either Islamic law or their cultural traditions.

    A.   Black Muslims

- African Americans who embrace Islam form a significant segment within the Muslim American community. However, they are not tightly organized into a single religious fellowship.
- Important leaders have been W. Fard Muhammad, Elijah Muhammad and, Malcolm X. Malcolm X was originally a member of the Nation of Islam and became the most powerful and brilliant voice of Black self-determination in the 1960s.
- Louis Farrakhan is the most recent spokesperson who led the 1995 Million Man March.

IV.   Immigration to the United States

- Spanish Muslims accompanied explorers and *conquistadores* to the Americans. Arabs immigrate as a result of encouragement from U.S.-funded missionary programs in the Middle East in the 19th century. The National Origins System slowed immigration and there was pressure to assimilate.
- In the Dearborn, Michigan area there is a great Arab presence. In 1919, the first mosque was established. Approximately forty percent of the Detroit, Michigan, area's population today is of Arab ancestry.
- The professional-preference clauses within the 1965 Immigration and Naturalization Act increased immigration among both Muslims and Arabs.

V.   Contemporary Life in the United States

    A.   Family Life and Gender

- Traditionally Islam permitted men to have multiple wives. Family patterns are more likely to be affected by the traditions of their homeland than by the fact that they are Muslim or Arab.
- Dress codes exist for both men and women. Women should wear head coverings. The *hijab* refers to a variety of garments that allow women to follow the guidelines of modest dress.
- Gender role differences are not limited to the home and the family. There are differences based within the faith and in the mosque or *masjid*. In many mosques there is segregation of the sexes.

    B.   Research Focus: Christian and Muslim Arab American Women's Gender Roles

    C.   Education

- Education is important. Schools are specific to particular expressions of Islam and specific nationalities.
- Children attending public schools may face the type of adjustment

experienced by those of a religious faith different from the dominant one of society. In districts with larger Muslim student populations, efforts have been made to recognize the religious diversity.

D.   Politics

- Muslims and Arab Americans are politically aware and often active. Muslims often express the view that their faith encourages political participation.
- U.S. politicians have begun to take the safe position of refusing campaign money from virtually any group linked to the Muslim or Arab community as charges have escalated that some Arab and Muslim community organizations and charities were giving money to groups who are anti-Israel or supportive of terrorist objectives.

VI.   Being Arab or Muslim in the United States

- Recent events have fueled anti-Arab and anti-Muslim feelings. For example, the 1972 Munich Olympic raid, the 1998, bombings of the U.S. embassies in Kenya and Tanzania, and the September 11, 2001 terrorists attacks.
- Racial profiling at airports and border checkpoints has moved into everyday life. The U.S. Department of Justice required that all foreign-born Muslim men were to be photographed, fingerprinted, and interviewed.
  A.   Listen to Our Voices: Pendulum Swings on Civil Rights

VII.   Issues of Prejudice and Discrimination

- Motion pictures show Muslims and Arabs as untrustworthy, savages, and barbaric. There is an overemphasis on the extreme representations of Arabs and Muslim Americans in the news and general information programming on television.
- Recent U.S. surveys found an increased willingness to view Muslims and Arabs as dangerous people who should carry special identification cards. Hate crimes and harassment toward Arab and Muslim Americans increased sharply since 9/11.
- Arab Americans and Muslim Americans have not been passive toward their treatment.

KEY TERMS

blended identity (p. 306)	hajj (p. 305)
hijab (p. 321)	jihad (p. 305)
Orientalism (p. 300)	deficit model of ethnic identity (p.303)

PRACTICE TESTS

Practice Test One

True-False
1.   T F   The Arab and Muslim American communities are among the slowest growing subordinate groups in the United States.
2.   T F   The hajj is a pilgrimage that is undertaken at least once in a lifetime to Mecca.
3.   T F   Many in the South saw making slaves Christians as part of their mission in civilizing the enslaved people.
4.   T F   Louis Farrakhan is known for his sharp attacks on other Black leaders, for his break with the Nation of Islam, and for his apparent shift to support the formation of coalitions with progressive Whites.
5.   T F   In 2003, there were 33 mosques in the metropolitan Detroit area, serving an estimated 200,000 Muslims.

Multiple Choice
1.   The single most unifying force among Arabs is
       A. religion.
       B. social class.
       C. the Prophet Muhammad.
       D. language.

2.   Among those identifying themselves as Arab America, the largest single source of ancestry is from
       A. Palestine.
       B. Egypt.
       C. Syria.
       D. Lebanon.

3.   Diversity underlies almost everything about Arab Americans. All of the following are discussed about their diversity in the chapter except
       A. the variation in religious tradition.
       B. the variation in language.
       C. the variation in the time of arrival to the United States.
       D. the variation in their point of origin.

4.   The world's largest religion is
       A. Christianity.
       B. Islam.
       C. Buddhism.
       D. Taoism.

5.   Muslims fast during the month of _____, which marks the revelation of the Qu'ran to the Prophet Muhammad.
A. Hajj
B. Sunnah
C. Sunnis
D. Ramadan

6.   The large majority of Muslims in the United States are _____ Muslims.
A. Shi'ia
B. Caliph
C. Sunni
D. Ka'aba

7.   Islam's authority rests with
A. the established hierarchy.
B. the scripture and the teachings of the Prophet.
C. the clergy in the mosque.
D. divine revelation.

8.   Roughly, the Arab background of Muslims in the United States is approximately
A. 20-42 percent.
B. 24-33 percent.
C. 12-32 percent.
D. 10-22 percent.

9.   _____ is the day marking the end of Ramadan.
A. Eid-al-Fitr
B. Shi'ia
C. Ka'aba
D. Sunniaba

10.   The simplistic view of the people and history of the Orient with no recognition of change over time or the diversity within its many cultures is
A. Occidentalism.
B. Maronitism.
C. Qumranism.
D. Orientalism.

Short-Answer Questions
1.   Explain the relationship between Muslim Americans and Arab Americans.
2.   Briefly describe the *deficit model of ethnic identity*.
3.   What is meant by the *blended identity of Muslim Americans*?
4.   Briefly describe the history of Black Muslims in the United States.
5.   Explain family life and gender roles in Muslim and Arab American families.

Practice Test Two

True-False

1. T F   Traditionally, Islam permitted men to have multiple wives--with a maximum of four.
2. T F   The *hijab* refers to a variety of garments that allow women to follow the guidelines of modest dress.
3. T F   The immediate aftermath of the 1995 bomb of the federal building in Oklahoma City showed the willingness of the public to accept stereotypes of Arab and Muslim Americans.
4. T F   The deficit model of ethnic identity concept is the self-image and worldview that is a combination of religious faith, cultural background based on nationality, and the status of being a resident of the United States.
5. T F   Arabs are an ethnic group and Muslims are a religious group.

Multiple Choice

1. There are approximately _____ mosques in the United States.
    A. 1,500
    B. 1,600
    C. 1,700
    D. 1,800

2. Approximately _____ percent of all African Americans are Islam.
    A. 5
    B. 10
    C. 15
    D. 20

3. The Nation of Islam became a well-known and controversial organization under the leadership of
    A. W. Fard Muhammad.
    B. Malcolm X.
    C. Spike Lee.
    D. Elijah Muhammad.

4. Another name for Malik El-Shabazz is
    A. W. Fard Muhammad.
    B. Malcolm X.
    C. Spike Lee.
    D. Elijah Muhammad.

5. The _____ restricted the number of Muslim immigrants to the United States.
   A. Repatriation Act
   B. National Origins System
   C. 1965 Immigration and Naturalization Act
   D. Patriot Act

6. _____ Muslim women should wear head coverings.
   A. Orthodox
   B. Ultra-orthodox
   C. Reformed
   D. Traditional

7. Mecca and Medina, the most holy mosques in Islam are located in
   A. Syria.
   B. Egypt.
   C. Lebanon.
   D. Saudi Arabia.

8. The research of _____ underscores the importance of considering immigrant status and commitment to one's faith.
   A. Qur'anic Muhazal
   B. Jawad al-Gheezi
   C. Jen'nan Ghazal Read
   D. Jahan Ghaemi

9. The American Muslim Alliance is a
   A. nonprofit organization.
   B. profit organization.
   C. public organization.
   D. private charity organization.

10. The motion picture _____ referred to Arabs as *barbaric*.
    A. The Mummy
    B. True Lies
    C. Aladdin
    D. The Mummy Returns

Short-Answer Questions
1. Explain the role of education for Muslim Americans.
2. How as being Arab or Muslim in the United States changed since 9/11?
3. Explain whether or not you think the Department of Justice has overreached its boundaries, since 9/11, by implementing several programs that have allegedly caused harm to Arab and Muslim immigrants and visitors to the United States.
4. Describe the differences between African American Muslims from other practicing Muslims in the United States.
5. Briefly describe hijab, hajj, and jihad.

ANSWERS TO PRACITCE TEST QUESTIONS

Practice Test One

True-False
1.   F (p. 300)
2.   T (p. 305)
3.   T (p. 308)
4.   F (p. 308)
5.   T (p. 311)

Multiple Choice
1.   D (p. 301)
2.   D (p. 303)
3.   B (p. 303)
4.   A (p. 304)
5.   D (p. 305)

6.   C (p. 301)
7.   B (p. 303)
8.   C (p. 304)
9.   A (p. 314)
10. D (p. 305)

Practice Test Two

True-False
1.   T (p. 312)
2.   T (p. 312)
3.   T (p. 316)
4.   F (p. 303)
5.   T (p. 300)

Multiple Choice
1.   C (p. 306)
2.   A (p. 307)
3.   D (p. 308)
4.   B (p. 309)
5.   B (p. 310)

6.   D (p. 312)
7.   D (p. 313)
8.   C (p. 313)
9.   A (p. 320)
10. C (p. 319)

APPLICATIONS/EXERCISES/ACTIVITIES

1.   What is the current standard of living for people of Arab ancestry in the United States? See the text and the following web site for appropriate information: http://www.census.gov/prod/2005pubs/censr-21.pdf

2.   Racial profiling or discriminatory police harassment is a frequent charge made by Muslim and Arab Americans as well as other minority groups. Learn more about racial profiling and the End Racial Profiling Act of 2004 by visiting: http://www.amnestyusa.org/racial_profiling/index.do

Chapter 11 – Muslim and Arab Americans: Diverse Minorities

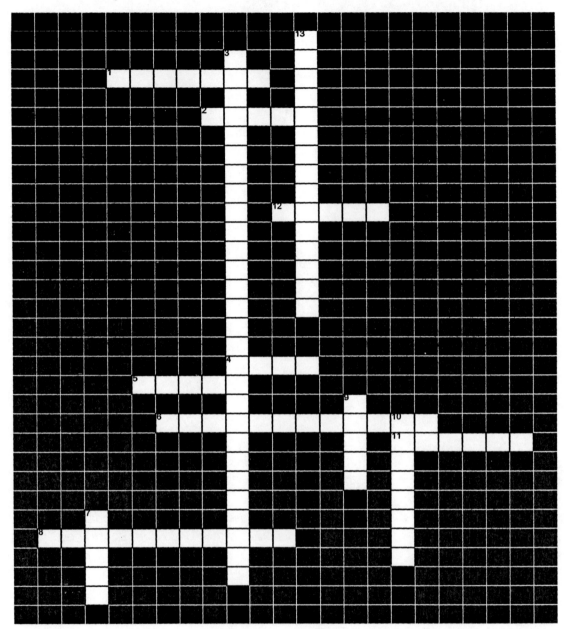

Across:
1   A place of worship
2   Struggle against the enemies of Allah, usually taken to mean one's own internal struggle
4   Pilgrimage to Mecca to be completed at least once in a Muslim's lifetime
5   Guides the teachings of Islam, which Muslims believe was revealed to the Prophet Muhammad
6   African Americans who are Muslim
8   The simplistic view of people and history of the Orient with no recognition of change over time or the diversity within its many cultures
11   A Muslim magazine
12   A city in contemporary Saudi Arabia

Down:
3   One's ethnicity is viewed by others as a factor or subtracting away the characteristics corresponding to some ideal ethnic type
7   A variety of garments that allow women to follow the guidelines of modest dress
9   The Muslim God
10   Is remembered for his sharp attacks on other Black leaders, for his break with the Nation of Islam, and for his shift to support the formation of coalitions with progressive Whites
13   Self-image and worldview that is a combination of religious faith, cultural background based on nationality, and current residency

Chapter Twelve

Asian Americans: Growth and Diversity

CHAPTER OBJECTIVES
- To understand that Asian Americans and Pacific Islanders are a diverse group and one of the fastest-growing segments of the U.S. population
- To understand the experience of Asian Americans in general and the experiences of Filipinos, Asian Indians, Southeast Asians, and Koreans in greater depth
- To explore the image of the "model minority" and how this stereotype impacts the life chances of Asian Americans
- To understand the current situation for Asian Americans in the areas of education and the economy
- To evaluate the idea that the door is half open for Asian Americans
- To gain an awareness of the political efforts of different Asian American populations as well as an to understand some of the reasons for the lack of political participation
- To gain an awareness of the experiences of Asian Indian immigrants to the U.S. and the unique situations that this group faces
- To gain an awareness of the experiences of Filipino immigrants to the U.S. and the unique situations that this group faces
- To explore the experiences of Southeast Asian American immigrants to the U.S. and the unique circumstances that this group faces
- To learn the ways in which Korean Americans have worked to move out of their subordinate status
- To gain an awareness of Hawaii and its people, understanding the factors that lead to its diversity as well as other issues that such a diversity presents

CHAPTER OUTLINE
I.   The "Model Minority" Image Explored
- The general image that people in the United States have of Asian Americans is that they represent a *model or ideal minority* because although they have experienced prejudice and discrimination, they seem to have succeeded economically, socially, and educationally without restoring to political or violent confrontation with Whites.
  A.   Education and the Economy
  - Asian Americans as a group have impressive school enrollment rates in comparison to the total population. In 2004, 49.4 percent of Asian Americans twenty-five years or older held bachelor's degrees.
  - That Asian Americans as a group have the same occupations as Whites suggests that they have been successful. However, Asian immigrants, like other minorities and immigrants before them, are found disproportionately in the low-paying service occupations. The absence of Asian Americans as top executives also indicates that their success is not complete.

- Asian Americans are typical of what sociologists call *middlemen minorities*, groups that occupy middle positions rather than positions at the bottom of the social scale, where many racial and ethnic minorities typically are located at least in the early years of residence here.
- Another sign of the apparent success of Asian Americans is their high incomes as a group. There are however striking contrasts in the earnings of Asian American families.
- The incorrect view of the "model minority" image is that it helps to exclude Asian Americans from social progress and conceals unemployment and social ills.

B. Listen To Our Voices: Being Pakistani, Muslim, and Female in America
C. The Door Half Open
- Asian Americans are victims of both prejudice and discrimination. The term *yellow peril* dates back to the view of Asian immigration.
- The news media use ethnic slurs and stereotypes, demonstrate insensitivity, and otherwise exhibit bias in reporting regarding Asian Americans. There are several ways in which this occurs, including, inappropriate use of clichés, mistaken identity, overgeneralization, ethnic slurs, inflammatory reporting, Japan bashing, media invisibility, and assumptions concerning Asian Americans being a model minority.
- The marginal status of Asian Pacific Islanders leaves them vulnerable to both selective and collective oppression, including *racial profiling*, or police-initiated action that relies on race, ethnicity, or national origin rather than the person's behavior.

II. Political Activity
- Asian Americans in general have not been more active in politics, including their geographic dispersal, a focus on getting ahead educationally and economically, and the need the use traits alien to many Asian cultures, such as being assertive and extolling one's virtues.
- Asian Americans are increasingly being regarded by both Republicans and Democrats as a future political force in the United States.

III. Diversity among Asian Americans
- The successive waves of immigrants to the United States from Asia and the Pacific Islands have been composed of a large number of nationalities and cultures.
- Asian Americans, like Native Americans, are not evenly distributed across the United States.

IV. Asian Indians
A. Immigration
- Like several other Asian immigrant groups, Asian Indians are recent immigrants. Only 17,000 immigrants came from 1820 to 1965, with the majority of those arriving prior to 1917. In the ten years after the 1965 Immigration Act more than 110,000 arrived.

- Three times the proportion of Asian Indian immigrants had a college degree compared to the general United States population. More recent immigrants, sponsored by earlier immigrant relatives, are displaying less facility with English, and the training they have tends to the less easily adapted to the U.S. workplace.

B. The Present Picture
- With more than 1 billion people in 2000, India is soon to be the most populous nation in the world.
- Parents are concerned about the erosion of traditional family authority among the desi. *Desi* is a colloquial name for people who trace their ancestry to South Asia, especially India and Japan.

C. Research Focus: Arranged Marriages in America

V. Filipino Americans
A. Immigration Patterns
- Four distinct periods of Filipino immigration are identified, including the first generation, immigrating in the 1920s who were mostly males who became employed in agricultural labor, a wave also arriving in the early twentieth century who immigrated to Hawaii, post-World War II war veterans and wives of United States soldiers, and the newest immigrants, including many professionals who arrived under the 1965 Immigration Act
- There is great diversity among Filipinos

B. The Present Picture
- More than two-thirds of the arrivals since the 1965 Immigration Act qualified for entry as professional and technical workers, but like Koreans, they have often worked at jobs below those they left in the Philippines.
- No significant single national Filipino social organization has formed for many reasons.

VI. Southeastern Asian Americans
A. The Refugees
- The *gook syndrome* is the tendency to stereotype Southeast Asians in the worst possible light.
- The primary objection to Vietnamese immigration was that it would further increase unemployment for Americans.

B. The Present Picture
- Most Southeast Asian immigrants look to the United States as their permanent home and the home of their children. Adult immigrants often accept jobs well below their occupational positions in Southeast Asia. Language is a factor in adjustment by refugees.
- The picture for young Southeast Asians in the U.S. is not completely pleasant.
- *Viet Kieu* refers to Vietnamese living abroad, who make a return to visit their homeland.

C. A Case Study: A Hmong Community
- The Hmong number about 186,000 in the United States today. Many immigrated to the United States from Laos and Vietnam after the April 1975 end of the United States involvement in Vietnam.
- In 2004, the United States recognized the special role that the Hmong people played in the Vietnam Conflict era. They agreed to accept thousands of Hmong people that had been in overseas refugee camps for thirty years.

VII. Korean Americans
A. Historical Background
- The population of Korean Americans in 2000 was one million. Today's Korean American community is the result of three waves of immigration. The initial wave was between 1903 and 1910. The second wave took place during and after the Korean War. The third wave was initiated by the passage of the 1965 Immigration Act.
- Korean Americans who accompanied their parents to the United States when young now occupy a middle, marginal position between the cultures of Korea and the United States. They have been called the *ilchomose*, or the "1.5 generation."
B. The Present Picture
- Today's young Korean Americans face many of the cultural conflicts common to any initial generation born in a new country. Korean American women commonly participate in the labor force, as do many other Asian American women.
- Korean American businesses are seldom major operations; most are small. They do benefit from a special form of development capital used to subsidize businesses, called a *kye*.
- In the early 1990s, nationwide attention was given to the friction between Korean Americans and other subordinate groups, primarily African Americans and Hispanics.
- Among Korean Americans the church is the most visible organization holding the group together. Half the immigrants were affiliated with Christian churches before immigrating.

VIII. Hawaii and Its People
- To grasp contemporary social relationships, we first must understand the historical circumstances that brought races together on the islands: the various Asian peoples and the *haoles*, the term often used to refer to Whites in Hawaii.
A. Historical Background
- Geographically remote, Hawaii was initially populated by Polynesian people, who had their first contact with Europeans in 1778. The Hawaiian people were united under a monarchy and received respect from the European immigrants. Slavery was never introduced.
- In 1893, a revolution encouraged by foreign commercial interests overthrew the monarchy. Five years later Hawaii was annexed as a

territory of the United States.
- The 1900 Organic Act guaranteed racial equality to Hawaiian people.

B. The Present Picture
- One clear of the multicultural nature of the islands is the degree of exogamy: marrying outside one's group.
- Equality between people is not absolute. Native Hawaiians tend to be least well off, working land they do not own. Haoles dominate the economy. The *AJAs* (Americans of Japanese ancestry, as they are called in Hawaii), are especially important in education, where they account for nearly fifty-eight percent of teachers, and in politics, where they dominate.
- Prejudice and discrimination are not alien to Hawaii. Attitudinal surveys show definite racial preferences and sensitivity to color differences.
- The *sovereignty movement* is the effort by the indigenous people of Hawaii to secure a measure of self-government and restoration of their lands.
- Hawaii is not a racial paradise. However, Hawaii's race relations are characterized more by harmony than by discord.

KEY TERMS

AJAs (p. 347)   model or ideal minority (p. 325)

desi (p. 335)   panethnicity (p. 348)

gook syndrome (p. 339)   racial profiling (p. 331)

Haoles (p. 345)   set-asides (p. 329)

ilchomose (p. 343)   sovereignty movement (p. 347)

kye (p. 344)   Viet Kieu (p. 341)

middlemen minorities (p. 328)   yellow peril (p. 330)

arranged marriages (p. 336)

PRACTICE TESTS

Practice Test One

True-False
1.   T F   Japanese Americans are the largest Asian group in the United States.
2.   T F   Social science literature considers Filipinos as Asians for geographic reasons, but physically and culturally they also reflect centuries of British rule.
3.   T F   With more than one billion people in 2000, India will soon become the most populous nation in the world.
4.   T F   Viet Kieu is a term referring to Vietnamese Americans, born in the United States, who return to live in their ancestors' homeland.
5.   T F   The largest Asian ethnic group represented in Hawaii is the Japanese.

Multiple Choice
1. Three of the following states have more than 500,000 Asian American residents. Which of the following states has fewer than 100,000?
   A. New York
   B. Alabama
   C. Texas
   D. California

2. Among Asian/Pacific Islanders, which of the following countries has the most people represented as Asian Americans?
   A. Korea
   B. Vietnam
   C. China
   D. Japan

3. The poverty rate for non-Hispanic Whites in 2002 was 8.2 percent. For Asian Americans it was _____ percent.
   A. 3.5
   B. 11.8
   C. 15.9
   D. 21.6

4. When a group experiences prejudice and discrimination, yet seems to have succeeded economically, socially, and educationally without resorting to political or violent confrontations with Whites, they are said to be a
   A. model minority.
   B. equitable minority.
   C. undiscriminated minority.
   D. winner minority.

5.   The gook syndrome refers to negative attitudes held by American of
      A. Mexicans.
      B. Asians.
      C. Cubans.
      D. Haitians.

6.   In 2004 what percent of Asians and Pacific Islanders living in the United States
      were not U.S. citizens?
      A. 12
      B. 23
      C. 34
      D. 45

7.   In the 2004 election most Asian Americans favored Democratic candidates. For
      Whites the percentage voting Democratic was _____ percent.
      A. 28
      B. 36
      C. 43
      D. 51

8.   Sociologist David Reisman has identified what he calls the _____ syndrome,
      referring to the tendency of stereotyping Asians in the worst possible light.
      A. Yellow plague
      B. Gook
      C. Wok
      D. Rice field

9.   About twenty-five percent of Wausau, Wisconsin's school children are of
      which Asian American group?
      A. Hmong
      B. Japanese
      C. Chinese
      D. Filipino

10.   The term used to refer to Whites in Hawaii is
      A. kye.
      B. ilchomose.
      C. Kiew.
      D. Haoles.

Short-Answer Questions
1.	What is the meaning of the term *model or ideal minority*?
2.	In what ways does the mass media exhibit insensitivity and bias toward Asian Americans?
3.	Identify the four distinct periods of Filipino immigration.
4.	What is meant by the term *Viet Kieu*?
5.	Briefly describe the *sovereignty movement*.

Practice Test Two

True-False
1.	T F	After the terrorist attacks of September 11th, 2001, anti-Asian violence increased dramatically for several months in the United States.
2.	T F	The primary language in the Philippines is *Tagalog*.
3.	T F	The largest influx of Asian Indians immigrants came to the United States prior to 1965.
4.	T F	The concept *ilchomose* refers to some Korean Americans.
5.	T F	The 1900 Organic Act guaranteed racial equality to the Hawaiian people.

Multiple Choice
1.	Hawaiians have experienced
	A. slavery.
	B. laws prohibiting interracial marriages.
	C. forced school segregation.
	D. none of the above.

2.	The sovereignty movement has as a goal to
	A. restore the land to native people.
	B. put in office a native Hawaiian government.
	C. see a return of the monarchy.
	D. achieve racial pluralism.

3.	Sociologists call Asian Americans a _____ *minority*.
	A. residual
	B. middlemen
	C. double-bind
	D. third-wave

4.	For every Asian American family earning more than $75,000 another earns _____.
	A. $50,000
	B. $30,000
	C. $20,000
	D. $10,000

5. Which of the following is not an example of a *Polynesian* Pacific Islander group?
   A. Native Hawaiian
   B. Samoan
   C. Hmong
   D. Tongan

6. The Philippines gained their independence in
   A. 1879.
   B. 1948.
   C. 1960.
   D. 1984.

7. The largest Asian American group is the Chinese. The second largest group is the
   A. Japanese.
   B. Korean.
   C. Samoan.
   D. Asian Indians

8. _____ is a colloquial name for people who trace their ancestry to south Asia, especially India and Japan.
   A. Haoles
   B. Ilchomose
   C. Kieu
   D. Desi

9. What percentage of the Hawaiian population in 2000 was "White?"
   A. 24
   B. 10
   C. 45
   D. 62

10. The _____ *movement* is the effort by the indigenous people of Hawaii to secure a measure of self-government and restoration of their lands.
    A. liberty
    B. Haoles
    C. sovereignty
    D. Pele

Short-Answer Questions
1. What is meant by the term *middlemen minority*?
2. What are four reasons why Asian Americans have not been particularly *politically active* in the United States?
3. Briefly describe the present picture of Asian Indians in the United States.
4. Describe the three waves of Korean immigration to the United States.
5. Describe the multicultural nature of the Hawaiian population.

ANSWERS TO PRACTICE TEST QUESTIONS

Practice Test One

True-False		Multiple Choice			
1.	F (p. 325)	1.	B (p. 325)	6.	C (p. 332)
2.	F (p. 335)	2.	C (p. 325)	7.	C (p. 333)
3.	T (p. 335)	3.	C (p. 328)	8.	B (p. 339)
4.	F (p. 341)	4.	A (p. 325)	9.	A (p. 341)
5.	T (p. 345)	5.	B (p. 339)	10.	D (p. 345)

Practice Test Two

True-False		Multiple Choice			
1	T (p. 329)	1.	D (p. 345)	6.	B (p. 336)
2	T (p. 337)	2.	A (p. 347)	7.	D (p. 325)
3	F (p. 334)	3.	B (p. 328)	8.	D (p. 343)
4	T (p. 343)	4.	D (p. 329)	9.	A (p. 345)
5	T (p. 346)	5.	C (p. 333)	10.	C (p. 347)

APPLICATIONS/EXERCISES/ACTIVITIES

1. In what ways has the Hmong immigration to the United States been functional and dysfunctional for the Hmong and for the United States? See the text and the following web site for appropriate information: http://www.stolaf.edu/people/cdr/hmong

2. Take a visit to your local travel agency. Get some vacation literature on Hawaii. How is race and ethnicity portrayed as a positive attribute unlike almost any other vacation destination in the United States?

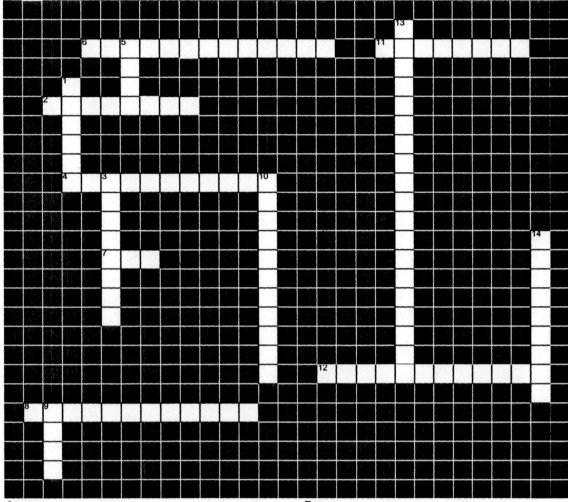

Across:
2   Type of union between man and woman that is arranged by parents
4   Tribal self-rule
6   A type of minority group that, despite past prejudice and discrimination, succeeds economically, socially, and educationally without resorting to political or violent confrontations with whites
7   Rotating credit system used by Korean Americans to subsidize the start of businesses
8   The development of solidarity between ethnic groups, as reflected in the terms Hispanic or *Asian Americans*
11   A subordinate group whose members have significantly less control or power over their own lives than do the members of a dominant or majority group
12   Americans' tendency to stereotype Asians and to regard them as all alike and undesirable

Down:
1   Hawaiian term for Caucasians
3   Vietnamese living abroad such as in the United States
5   Colloquial name for people who trace their ancestry to South Asia, especially India and Pakistan
9   Americans of Japanese ancestry in Hawaii
10   A term denoting a generalized prejudice toward Asian people and their customs
13   Groups such as Japanese Americans that typically occupy middle positions in the social and occupational stratification strategy
14   Programs stipulating that a minimum proportion of government contracts must be awarded to minority-owned businesses

Chapter Thirteen

Chinese Americans and Japanese Americans

CHAPTER OBJECTIVES

- To learn that present-day Chinese Americans are descendants of both pre-Exclusion Act immigrants and those who immigrated after World War II
- To understand the occupational profile of Chinese Americans
- To learn what life is like inside Chinatown
- To understand the family and religious life of Chinese Americans
- To learn about the migration of Chinese people to the U.S.
- To understand the historical situation of Japanese Americans in the U.S
- To understand and evaluate how Japanese Americans encountered discrimination and ill treatment in the early twentieth century
- To explore the wartime evacuation experience of Japanese Americans during World War II
- To learn about the economic picture of Japanese Americans today
- To understand the family and religious life of Japanese Americans
- To explore and evaluate the remnants of prejudice and discrimination of Chinese and Japanese Americans in the U.S.

CHAPTER OUTLINE

I. Chinese Americans
- From the beginning of Chinese immigration, Americans have held conflicting views about it. Chinese immigration brought hard-working laborers, but also an alien culture.
- The anti-Chinese mood led to the passage of the Exclusion Act of 1882, which was repealed in 1943. Very gradually Chinese were permitted to enter the United States after 1943.
   A. Occupational Profile of Chinese Americans
   - Chinese Americans have lower unemployment rates and are better represented in professional occupations than the population as a whole. The backbone of the contemporary Chinese American labor force still lies though in Chinatown.
   B. Chinatowns Today
   - Chinatowns represent a paradox. The casual observer or tourist sees them as thriving areas of business and amusement. Behind the facade, however, they have large poor populations and face the problems associated with all slums.
   - The Chinese in this country have a rich history of organizational membership, much of it carried over from China. Chief among such associations as the clans, or *tsu*; the benevolent associations, or *hui kuan*; and the secret societies, or *tongs*.
   - The tourist industry is a double-edged sword. It does provide needed jobs.

But it also forces Chinatown to keep its problems quiet and not seek outside assistance, lest tourists hear of social problems and stop coming.

- The social problems have grown more critical as Chinese immigration has increased.
- The attacks on the World Trade Center in 2001 made the marginal economy of New York's China Town even shakier.
- Increasingly, Chinese Americans neither live nor work in Chinatowns. The movement of Chinese Americans out of Chinatowns parallels the movement of White ethnics out of similar enclaves.

C.   Family and Religious Life

- For Chinese Americans, the latest immigration wave has helped preserve some of the old ways, but traditional cultural patterns have undergone change even in the People's Republic of China, so the situation is very fluid.
- The contemporary Chinese American family is basically indistinguishable from its White counterpart except that it is victimized by prejudice and discrimination.
- Where acculturation has taken hold less strongly, Chinese Americans the legacy of China remains.
- Another problem for Chinese Americans is the rise in gang activity since the mid-1970s.

D.   Research Focus: Chinese Christians or Christian Chinese?

II.   Japanese Americans

- Japanese Americans distinguish sharply between themselves according how long a person's family has been in the United States. The *Issei* are the first generation, the immigrants born in Japan. Their children, the *Nesei* are American-born. The third generation, the *Sansei*, must go back to their grandparents to reach their roots in Japan. The *Yonsei* are the fourth generation. Some Nisei are sent by their parents to Japan for schooling and to have marriages arranged, after which they return to the United States. Japanese Americans expect such people, called *Kibei*, to be less acculturated than other Nisei.

A.   The Wartime Evacuation

- On February 13, 1942, President Franklin Roosevelt signed Executive Order 9066. It defined strategic military areas in the United States and authorized the removal from those areas of any people considered threats to national security.
- Merely having a Japanese great-grandparent was enough to mark a person for involuntary confinement in an internment camp.
- Even before reaching the camps, the *evacuees*, as Japanese Americans being forced to resettle came to be called officially, paid the price for their ancestry.
- Ten camps were established in seven states. The Japanese Americans did not go there voluntarily, they had been charged with no crime, and they could not leave without official approval. Japanese Americans were able to work at wage labor in the camps.

- A loyalty test was administered in 1943 on a form all had to fill out, the "Application for Leave Clearance."
- Finally, the Supreme Court ruled on December 18, 1944, that the detainment was unconstitutional.
- The wartime evacuation cost the United States taxpayers a quarter of a billion dollars in construction, transportation, and military expenses. Japanese Americans effectively lost at least several billion dollars.
- Racism cannot be ignored as an explanation. Japanese Americans were placed in camps, but German Americans and Italian Americans were largely ignored.
- A commission recommendation in 1983 was that the government should formally apologize to Japanese Americans and give $20,000 tax-free to each of the approximately 82,000 surviving internees. Congress began hearings in 1986 on the bill authorizing these steps, and President Reagan signed the Civil Liberties Act of 1988.

B. The Economic Picture
- The Japanese American community is more settled and less affected by new arrivals from the home country than are Chinese Americans. Japanese Americans are doing very well. The educational attainment of Japanese Americans as a group. Their family earnings are higher than that of Whites. Japanese Americans have achieved success by overcoming barriers that United States society had created.
- The most dramatic development has been the upward mobility that they have collectively and individually accomplished.

C. Family and Religious Life
- As cultural traditions fade the contemporary Japanese American family seems to continue the success story.
- As is true of the family and other social organizations, religious life in these groups has its antecedents in Asia, but there is no single Japanese faith. Although traditional temples are maintained in most places where there are large numbers of Japanese Americans, many exist only as museums, and few are places of worship with growing memberships.

D. Listen To Our Voices: From Kawasaki to Chicago

III. Remnants of Prejudice and Discrimination
- In popular television series, Asian Americans, if they are present, usually are either karate experts or technical specialists involved in their work Chinese Americans are ignored or misrepresented in history books.
- The intermarriage rate for Japanese Americans is high, with two-thirds of all children born to a Japanese American had a parent of a different race. The Japanese American community struggles to maintain its cultural identity.
- It is important to not interpret assimilation as an absence of protest.

KEY TERMS

evacuees (p. 361)   Sansei (p. 359)   Nisei (p. 359)

hui kuan (p. 355)   tongs (p. 355)

Issei (p. 359)   tsu (p. 354)

Kibei (p. 359)   Yonsei (p. 359)

PRACTICE TESTS

Practice Test One

True-False
1.   T F   Over the past twenty years the population of Chinese Americans has actually been declining.
2.   T F   In the People's Republic of China, organized religion barely exists.
3.   T F   A Japanese submarine actually attacked a California oil tank complex in early 1943.
4.   T F   Less than one-half of Japanese Americans in 1940 lived on the west coast of the United States.
5.   T F   New York City has ten times more Asian Pacific Islanders than does Seattle.

Multiple Choice
1.   Today, there are approximately 2.3 million Chinese Americans. How many Japanese Americans are there?
      A. .8 million
      B. 1.5 million
      C. 2.4 million
      D. 3.9 million

2.   The background of the contemporary Chinese American labor force lies in
      A. Chinatowns.
      B. farming.
      C. steel mills.
      D. factories.

3.   The Chinese in this country have a rich history of organizational membership. Chief among such associations are the *clans*, or _____.
      A. Tongs
      B. Nisei
      C. Kibei
      D. Tsu

4.   The Chinese have also organized in _____, or *secret societies*.
      A. Tsu
      B. Nisei
      C. Kuan
      D. Tongs

5.   The first generation of Japanese in the United States is called _____.
      A. Nisei
      B. Yonsei
      C. Issei
      D. Kibei

6.   Japanese Americans who were sent to evacuation or internment camps were
      called _____.
      A. Sansei
      B. Kamans
      C. Ilchomes
      D. evacuees

7.   The Civil Liberties Act of 1988 dealt with
      A. Chinese Americans.
      B. Japanese Americans.
      C. Korean Americans.
      D. All Asian Americans.

8.   Census data shows that _____ of all children born to a Japanese Americans
      had a parent of a different race.
      A. one-sixth
      B. one-eighth
      C. two-thirds
      D. one-half

9.   Executive Order 9066 covered _____ percent of Japanese Americans on the
      mainland.
      A. 60
      B. 70
      C. 80
      D. 90

10.   Which of the following cities has the largest population of Asian Americans?
      A. Los Angeles
      B. Chicago
      C. New York City
      D. Seattle

Short-Answer Questions

1. What conclusions are being drawn by the author concerning Chinese American social organizations?
2. Summarize the occupational profile of Chinese Americans.
3. In what ways do you think Chinese and Japanese Americans are being stereotyped in the mass media today?
4. Describe the nature of the Japanese American internment camps during World War II.
5. Differentiate between *tongs* and *hui kuan*.

Practice Test Two

True-False

1. T F The *Sansei* are more heterogeneous than their *Nisei* and *Issei* relatives.
2. T F At no point in United States history has Japanese Americans outnumbered Chinese Americans.
3. T F Most Christian Chinese are Protestant.
4. T F The Issei refers to all American born Japanese Americans.
5. T F The educational attainment of Japanese Americans as a group, as well as their family earnings, is higher than that for Whites.

Multiple Choice

1. Women in Chinatown
   A. are not allowed to learn English.
   B. often work in the garment industry sweatshops.
   C. dominate the legal profession.
   D. are more likely to have non-Chinese husbands.

2. The Chinese Exclusion Act of 1882 was repealed in
   A. 1891.
   B. 1917.
   C. 1943.
   D. 1965.

3. Benevolent Chinese organizations are known as
   A. hui kuan.
   B. tongs.
   C. tsu.
   D. Kesei.

4.   The _____ are the offspring of Japanese immigrants who were born in Japan.
      A. Issei
      B. Nisei
      C. Yonsei
      D. Kibei

5.   Some Nisei are sent back to Japan by their parents for schooling and to have marriages arranged, after which they return to the United States. They are called _____.
      A. Sansei
      B. Issei
      C. Kibei
      D. Nansi

6.   Which of the following defined the strategic military areas in the United States and authorized the removal from those areas of any people considered threats to national security?
      A. The North American Protection Act
      B. Executive Order 9066
      C. The Immigration Act of 1965
      D. The Defense Act of 1941

7.   Which of the following states did not have an evacuation camp for Japanese Americans during World War II?
      A. Arizona
      B. California
      C. Arkansas
      D. New York

8.   The Japanese Americans evacuation camps were located in _____.
      A. California
      B. California and Arizona
      C. seven states
      D. all 48 states

9.   Internment camps during World War II illustrate
      A. segregation.
      B. expulsion.
      C. assimilation.
      D. pluralism.

10.   The Chinese phrase *Zhancan zhugen* means
      A. to forget the past means to repeat it.
      B. to be but not do is unthinkable.
      C. you can never step in the same river twice.
      D. to eliminate the weeds, one must pull out the roots.

Short-Answer Questions

1. What does the author mean by saying that Chinatowns represent a paradox?
2. What role do Chinatowns play for Chinese Americans?
3. Differentiate between *assimilation patterns* of Chinese Americans and Japanese Americans.
4. What are the new social problems confronting residents of Chinatowns?
5. What are two conclusions being made by the author concerning Chinese and Japanese Americans?

ANSWERS TO PRACTICE TEST QUESTIONS

Practice Test One

True-False		Multiple Choice			
1.	F (p. 352)	1.	A (p. 352)	6.	D (p. 361)
2.	T (p. 357)	2.	A (p. 353)	7.	B (p. 363)
3.	T (p. 360)	3.	D (p. 354)	8.	C (p. 368)
4.	F (p. 360)	4.	B (p. 355)	9.	D (p. 360)
5.	T (p. 369)	5.	C (p. 359)	10.	C (p. 369)

Practice Test Two

True-False		Multiple Choice			
1.	T (p. 359)	1.	B (p. 356)	6.	B (p. 360)
2.	F (p. 352)	2.	C (p. 353)	7.	D (p. 360)
3.	T (p. 358)	3.	A (p. 355)	8.	C (p. 360)
4.	F (p. 359)	4.	B (p. 359)	9.	B (p. 368)
5.	T (p. 364)	5.	C (p. 359)	10.	D (p. 370)

APPLICATIONS/EXERCISES/ACTIVITIES

1.   Information about the Chinese Exclusion Act can be found by following these steps. Log onto the site (http://www.google.com), and type the words "Chinese Exclusion Act" into the search box. Press the search key, and you will be provided with numerous links to the act. Read several and use the functionalist perspective and conflict theory to explain the reasons for and the consequences of this act.

2.   Watch television for two hours. Critically evaluate the commercials, the program characters and the role behaviors of the actors. Summarize your results by addressing the following issues:
   - Are all of the racial and ethnic groups represented equally?
   - What roles do minority group members have? Do they share common characteristics?
   - What roles do majority group members have? Do they share any common characteristics?
   - What conclusions can you make about your little experiment?
   - What suggestions could your give to television producers, media advertisers, etc. about exposing our society to racial and ethnic stereotyping?

Chapter 13 – Chinese Americans and Japanese Americans

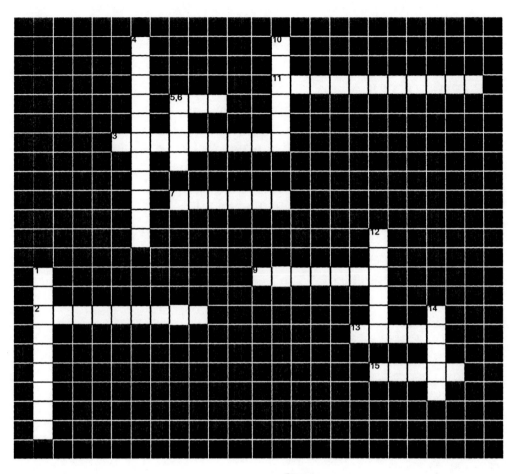

Across:

2 Mutual respect between the various groups in a society for one another's cultures, allowing minorities to express their own culture without experiencing prejudice or hostility

3 In the inner-city where the majority of the people are of Chinese ancestry

6 Clans established along family lines and forming a basis for social organization by Chinese Americans

7 The children of the Nisei--that is, the grandchildren of the original immigrants from Japan

9 Chinese American benevolent associations organized on the basis of the district of the immigrant's origin in China

11 The physical separation of two groups, often imposed on a subordinate group by the dominant group

13 Children born of immigrants from Japan

15 First-generation immigrants from Japan to the United States

Down:

1 Examples include Japanese Camps during World War II, the ethnic Chinese from Vietnam in the 1970s

4 Where the Japanese bombed the United States at the beginning of World War II

5 Chinese American secret associations

10 A minority and a majority group combining to form a new group

12 The fourth generation of Japanese Americans in the United States; the children of the Sansei

14 Japanese Americans of the Nisei generation sent back to Japan for schooling and to have marriages arranged

Chapter Fourteen

Jewish Americans: Quest to Maintain Identity

CHAPTER OBJECTIVES
- To understand the Jewish people are an ethnic group.
- To understand that their identity rests not on the presence of physical traits or religious beliefs but on a sense of belonging that is tied to Jewish ancestry
- To explore distinctive aspects of the Jewish population
- To gain an understanding of the migration patterns of Jewish people to the U.S. and how this has influenced the formation of a Jewish identity
- To learn of the origins and impacts of anti-Semitism on the lives and culture of Jewish people
- To compare and contrast anti-Semitism inside and outside of the United States
- To gain an understanding of the present situation of Jewish people in the United States with regard to their employment, education, organizational activity, and political activity
- To explore the religious life of Jewish Americans focusing on both the Orthodox tradition and Reform tradition
- To gain an understanding of the importance of the role of the family, the role of religion, and the role of cultural heritage in forming Jewish identity and Jewish culture in the U.S.

CHAPTER OUTLINE
I.   The Jewish People: Race, Religion, or Ethnic Group?
- The United States has the largest Jewish population in the world. Unlike many other subordinate groups, Jewish cultural heritage is not nationalistic in origin. Perhaps the most striking difference is that the history of anti-Jewish prejudice and discrimination (usually called *anti-Semitism)* is nearly as old as relations between Jews and Gentiles (non-Jews).
- Jews are a subordinate group because they fulfill the criteria set forth in Chapter 1.
- What are the distinguishing traits for Jewish Americans? The issue of what makes a Jew is not only a scholarly question; in Israel it figures in policy matters. The Israel Law of Return defines who is a Jew and extends Israeli citizenship to all Jews.
- The Jewish people are not physically differentiated from non-Jews. Jews come from all areas of the world and carry a variety of physical features.
- To be a Jewish American does not mean that one is affiliated with one of the three religious groups: the Orthodox, the Reform, and the Conservative.
- The trend for some time, especially in the United States, has been toward a condition called *Judaization,* the lessening importance of Judaism as a religion and the substitution of cultural tradition as the ties that bind Jews.
- The question of what constitutes Jewish identity is not easily resolved.

II.   Immigration of Jews to the United States
- One of the most significant movements among Jews is the one that created history's largest concentration of Jews: the immigration to the United States. The first Jews arrived in 1654. When the United States gained its independence from Great Britain, only 2,500 Jews lived here. The greatest migration of Jews to the United States occurred around the end of the nineteenth century.
- Despite the legacy of anti-Semitism in Europe, past and present, most of the Jews who migrated to the United States up to the early twentieth century came voluntarily. The immigration acts of the 1920s sharply reduced the influx of Jews, as they did that of other European groups.
- Because the Immigration and Naturalization Service does not identify an immigrant's religion, precise data are lacking for the number of people of Jewish background migrating recently to the United States.

III.   Anti-Semitism Past and Present
A.   Origins
- Many anti-Semites justify their beliefs by pointing to the role of some Jews in the crucifixion of Jesus Christ.
- The myth of Jews being fixated on money may be explained by Gordon Allport's *fringe of values theory*. According to this theory, throughout history Jews have occupied positions economically different from those of Gentiles, often because laws forbade them to farm or practice trades.
- A similar explanation is given for other stereotypes, such as the assertion that Jews are clannish, staying among themselves and not associating with others.
- Being critical of others for traits for which you praise members of your own group is an example of the *in-group virtues* becoming *out-group vices*.
B.   The Holocaust
- The *Holocaust* is the state sponsored systematic persecution and annihilation of European Jewry by Nazi Germany and its collaborators.
- Despite the enormity of the tragedy, a small but vocal proportion of the world's community are *Holocaust revisionists* who claim that the Holocaust did not happen.
- Anti-Semitism is definitely not just a historical social phenomenon in Europe.
C.   Listen To Our Voices: "Night"
D.   United States: Anti-Semitism: Past
- In 1654, the year Jews arrived in colonial America, Peter Stuyvesant, governor of New Amsterdam (the Dutch city later named New York), attempted to expel them from the city.
- The 1920s and the 1930s were a period of the most virulent and overt ant-Semitism. In these decades, the myth of an internationally

organized Jewry took shape. According to a forged document titled *Protocols of the Elders of Zion*, Jews throughout the world planned to conquer all governments, and the major vehicle for this rise to power was communism. Henry Ford had the *Protocols* published in a weekly newspaper he owned.

- Unlike its European counterparts, the United States government has never embarked on an anti-Semitic program of expulsion or extermination.

E. Contemporary Anti-Semitism

- The Anti-Defamation League of B'nai B'rith, founded in 1913, makes an annual survey of reported anti-Semitic incidents. There were 1,757 incidents in 2005. Particularly disturbing has been the number of reported anti-Semitic incidents on college campuses.

- Although not all American Jews agree with Israel's actions, many Jews express support for Israel's struggles by contributing money and trying to influence America's opinion and policy to be more favorable to Israel.

- *Zionism*, which initially referred to the old Jewish religious yearning to return to the biblical homeland, has been expressed in the twentieth century in the movement to create a Jewish state in Palestine. Ever since the *Diaspora*, the exile of Jews from Palestine several centuries before Christianity, many Jews have seen the destiny of their people only as the establishment of a Jewish state in the Holy Land.

- In 1974 the United Nations General Assembly passed a resolution declaring the "Zionism is a form of racism and racial discrimination." The Zionism resolution, finally repealed by the UN in 1991, had no lasting influence and did not change any nation's foreign policy.

- The contemporary anti-Semitism of African Americans is of special concern to Jewish Americans. Surveys do not necessarily show significant differences between Blacks and Whites in anti-Semitism.

- African American resentment has rarely been anti-Jewish, but rather, as opposed to White institutions.

IV. Position of Jewish Americans

A. Employment and Income

- Jews have experienced, and to a limited extent still experience, differential treatment in the American job market.

- Using a variety of techniques, social science studies have documented declining discrimination against Jews in the business world.

- The overall economic success of Jews obscures the poverty of many individual Jewish families.

B. Education

- Jews place great emphasis on education. Seventy-six percent of Jews have received some form of formal Jewish education before they reach 30 years of age.

- Jews have a value system that stresses education.

C.	Organizational Activity
- The American Jewish community has encompassed a variety of organizations since its beginnings. These groups have many purposes, including religious and charitable. Besides national groups there are many community-based groups very active.

D.	Political Activity
- American Jews play a prominent role in politics as both voters and elected officials. Jews as a group are not typical in that they are more likely than the general population to label themselves as liberal.
- As in all subordinate groups, the political activity of Jewish Americans has not been limited to conventional electoral politics. Radical Jewish politics has been dominated by college students.

V.	Religious Life
- Jewish identity and participation in the Jewish religion are not the same.
- The Judaic faith embraces a number of factions or denominations that are similar in their roots but marked by sharp distinctions. Seven percent of Jews identify themselves as Orthodox, twenty-nine percent as Conservative, two percent as Reconstructionist, twenty-nine percent as Reform, and thirty-three percent as just Jewish.

A.	The Orthodox Tradition
- The unitary Jewish tradition developed in the United States into three sects, beginning in the mid-nineteenth century. The differences between Orthodox, Conservative, and Reform Judaism are based on their varying acceptance of traditional rituals.
- Orthodox Jewish life is very demanding, especially in a basically Christian society such as the United States. Almost all conduct is defined by rituals that require reaffirmation of religious conviction constantly. Most Americans are familiar with *kashrut*, the laws pertaining to permissible and forbidden foods.

B.	The Reform Tradition
- Reform Jews, though deeply committed to the religious faith, have altered many of the rituals.
- Unlike most faiths in the United States, Jews have historically have not embarked on recruitment or evangelistic programs to attract new members.
- The Reform Jews are the wealthiest and have the best formal education of the group.
- A fourth branch of American Judaism, Reconstructionism, an offshoot of the Conservative movement, has only recently developed an autonomous institutional structure with ritual practices similar to those of Reform Jews.
- *Table 14.2* (p. 392) displays some results of a national survey on Jewish identity.

VI.   Jewish Identity
  - Improved relations with Gentiles have made it possible for Jews to shed their "Jewishness," or *Yiddishkait*.
  - A unique identity issue presents itself to Jewish women, whose religious tradition has placed them in a subordinate position. The have been some changes to *halakha* (Jewish law covering obligations and duties), but it is still difficult for a woman to get a divorce recognized by Orthodox Jewish tradition.
  A.   Role of the Family
    - For religious Jews the family fulfills a religious commandment. In the past this compulsion was so strong that the *shadchan* (the marriage broker or matchmaker) fulfilled an important function in the Jewish community by ensuring marriage for all eligible people.
    - Ten problems with contemporary Jewish families have been identified by the Jewish American Committee. Of the ten, intermarriage has received the greatest attention from Jewish leaders.
  B.   Research Focus: Intermarriage: The Final Step to Assimilation?
  C.   Role of Religion
    - The religious question facing Jews is not so much one of ideology as of observing the commandments of traditional Jewish law. *Marginality* describes the status of living in two distinct cultures simultaneously. Jews who give some credence to the secular aspects of Christmas celebrations exemplify individuals' accommodating themselves to two cultures.
  D.   Role of Cultural Heritage
    - For many Jews, religious observance is a very small aspect of their Jewishness.
    - Yiddish is only one of many languages spoken by some Jews.
    - *Peoplehood* refers to a group with a shared feeling. For Jews this sense of identity originates from a variety of sources, past and present, both within and without.

KEY TERMS

anti-Semitism (p. 374)   Judaization (p. 376)

Diaspora (p. 385)   kashrut (p. 391)

fringe-of-values theory (p. 379)   marginality (p. 396)

halakha (p. 393)   Zionism (p. 385)

Holocaust (p. 381)   peoplehood (p. 398)

Holocaust revisionist (p. 381)   Yiddoshkait (p. 393)

in-group virtues (p. 380)   out-group vices (p. 380)

PRACTICE TESTS

Practice Test One

True-False
1. T F   The United States has the largest Jewish population in the world.
2. T F   The Israel Law of Return defines who is a Jew and extends Israeli citizenship to all Jews.
3. T F   *Judaization* refers to the process through which Jews learn Talmudic Law.
4. T F   *Reform Jews* generally are not as financially well-off as Orthodox or Conservative
5. T F   *Yiddish* is a language that first emerged in the United States during the late nineteenth century in the midst of the great European immigration period.

Multiple Choice
1. The author identifies the Jews as a _____ group.
    A. superordinate
    B. residual
    C. subordinate
    D. latent

2. The first Jews arrived in the United States in
    A. 1654.
    B. 1820.
    C. 1492.
    D. 1759.

3. If the stereotype that Jews are obsessed with money is false, how did it originate? Gordon Allport has advanced the _____ theory suggesting that historically Jews have occupied positions economically different from those of Gentiles, often because laws forbade them to farm or practice trades.
    A. out-group vices
    B. in-group virtues
    C. Diaspora
    D. fringe-of-values

4. What were the Protocols?
    A. beliefs based on Zionism
    B. Talmudic Law
    C. a forged anti-Semitic document
    D. kosher laws

5. The exile of Jews from Palestine several centuries before Christianity is known as the _____
    A. Diaspora
    B. Exodus
    C. kashrut
    D. kiddish

6. While twenty-eight percent of the Jews in the United States identify themselves as "moderate" in terms of ideology, what percentage say they are "liberal"?
    A. 21
    B. 46
    C. 12
    D. 33

7. What percentage of Jews in the United States are affiliated with a synagogue?
    A. 44
    B. 46
    C. 12
    D. 57

8. *Kashrut* refers to
    A. Jews who do not follow the Sabbath.
    B. the ideology of Jews as a "chosen" people.
    C. laws pertaining to permissible and forbidden foods.
    D. "Jewishness."

9. Which of the following does not characterize Jews in the United States today?
    A. birth rates are rising
    B. divorce rates are rising
    C. intermarriage has lessened the involvement of the Jewish partner in Jewish life
    D. there is less socializing across generational lines, partly as a result of geographic development

10. *Yiddishkait* refers to
    A. laws regarding forbidden foods.
    B. Jewishness.
    C. Talmudic Law.
    D. laws covering obligations and duties.

Short-Answer Questions

1. Differentiate between the Orthodox and Reform traditions among Jewish Americans.
2. The American Jewish Committee has identified ten problems that are endangering the family as the main transmission agent of Jewish values, identity, and continuity. What are four of these problems?
3. What is the evidence for anti-Semitism in the United States today?

4. What does the author mean by saying that Jewish identity and participation with Jewish religion are not the same thing?

5. Briefly describe the general patterns of political activity and ideology among Jewish Americans.

Practice Test Two

True-False
1. T F Florida has the largest population of Jewish people in the United States.
2. T F By law, the Immigration and Naturalization Service must identify an immigrant's religion.
3. T F Unlike its European counterparts, the United States government has never embarked on an anti-Semitic program of expulsion or extermination.
4. T F Most Jews in the United States identify themselves as *Republicans*.
5. T F According to the author, the religious question facing Jews is not so much about observing the commandments of traditional Jewish law, but one of ideology.

Multiple Choice
1. Which of the following states has the largest Jewish population?
    A. California
    B. New York
    C. Florida
    D. Illinois

2. The lessening importance of Judaism as a religion and the substitution of cultural traditions as the ties that bind Jews.
    A. Judaization
    B. Protocols
    C. Diaspora
    D. Zionism

3. Holocaust revisionists
    A. spearheaded the Holocaust memorial in Washington, D.C.
    B. work through the year to incorporate information about the Holocaust in public education to ensure that "we never forget."
    C. claim the Holocaust did not happen.
    D. have worked to ensure that the perpetrators of the Holocaust are brought to justice.

4. *Kristallnacht* means
    A. the night of believing.
    B. the night of rest and faith.
    C. the night of lights.
    D. the night of broken glass.

5.   Fifteen percent of U.S. workers have professional occupations. What is the corresponding percentage for Jewish workers?
        A. 20
        B. 40
        C. 60
        D. 80

6.   What percentage of Jewish people in the United States over the age of twenty-five has a college degree?
        A. 24
        B. 37
        C. 59
        D. 73

7.   What percentage of Jewish Americans identifies themselves as *Orthodox*?
        A. 7
        B. 19
        C. 27
        D. 46

8.   Which of the following is inaccurate about *Reform Jews*?
        A. women and men sit together in congregations
        B. circumcision is mandatory for males
        C. civil divorce decrees are sufficient
        D. children of non-Jewish women and Jewish men are recognized as Jews with no need to convert

9.   _____ refers to Jewish law covering obligations and duties.
        A. Kashrut
        B. Yiddish
        C. Halakha
        D. Kait

10.   _____ houses are both social and spiritual gathering places for Jewish students on college campuses.
        A. Hillel
        B. Goldstein
        C. Kashrut
        D. Halakha

Short-Answer Questions
1.   In what ways are Jews a *subordinate group*?
2.   Briefly describe the immigration of Jews to the United States.
3.   Briefly describe the worldwide distribution of Jews.

4.   What does Robert Merton mean that in-group virtues become out-group vices?
5.   Describe the relative position of Jewish Americans in terms of employment, income, and education.

ANSWERS TO PRACTICE TEST QUESTIONS

Practice Test One

True-False   **Multiple Choice**
1.   T (p. 374)   1.   C (p. 376)   6.   B (p. 387)
2.   T (p. 376)   2.   A (p. 377)   7.   B (p. 389)
3.   F (p. 376)   3.   D (p. 379)   8.   C (p. 391)
4.   F (p. 392)   4.   C (p. 383)   9.   A (p. 394)
5.   F (p. 398)   5.   A (p. 385)   10.   B (p. 393)

Practice Test Two

True-False   **Multiple Choice**
1.   F (p. 375)   1.   B (p. 376)   6.   C (p. 387)
2.   F (p. 378)   2.   A (p. 376)   7.   A (p. 390)
3.   T (p. 383)   3.   C (p. 381)   8.   B (p. 397)
4.   F (p. 387)   4.   D (p. 381)   9.   C (p. 393)
5.   F (p. 377)   5.   B (p. 387)   10.   A (p. 397)

APPLICATIONS/EXERCISES/ACTIVITIES

1.   Use functionalist theory to explain the role played by Jewish Americans during the United States Civil War using information presented at the following web site: http://www.civilwarhome.com/jewish.htm to support your argument.

2.   Write a short paper discussing how the treatment of Jews in Europe was comparable to the treatment of African Americans under the Jim Crow laws.

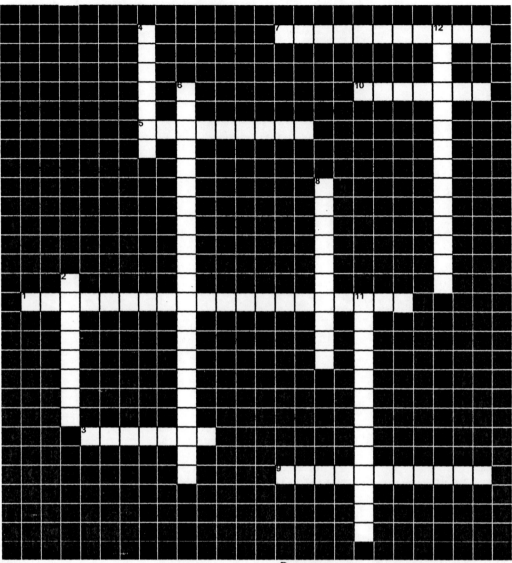

Across:

1 Behavior that is on the border of conduct that a society regards as proper and is often carried out by subordinate groups, subjecting those groups to negative sanctions

3 Traditional Jewish religious yearning to return to the biblical homeland, now used to refer to support for the state of Israel

5 The state-sponsored systematic persecution and annihilation of European Jewry by Nazi Germany and its collaborators

7 The lessening importance of Judaism as a religion and the substitution of cultural traditions as the tie that binds Jews

9 The status of being between two cultures at the same time, such as the status of Jewish immigrants in the United States

10 Laws pertaining to permissible (kosher) and forbidden foods and their preparation

Down:

2 The exile of Jews from Palestine

4 Jewish laws covering obligations and duties

6 People who deny the Nazi effort to exterminate the Jews or who minimize the numbers killed

8 A group with a shared feeling

11 Proper behavior by one's own group (in group virtues) becomes unacceptable when practiced by outsiders (out-group vices)

12 Proper behavior by one's own group (in-group virtues) becomes unacceptable when practiced by outsiders (out-group vices)

Chapter Fifteen

Women: The Oppressed Majority

CHAPTER OBJECTIVES
- To understand that women are an oppressed group even though they form the numerical majority
- To understand and evaluate the similarities between women and racial and ethnic groups
- To evaluate how socialization has an impact on the development and perception of gender roles
- To understand the impact of gender roles in perpetuating inequalities between men and women
- To learn and evaluate how conflict theory, functional theory, and labeling theory explain gender role socialization
- To explore the historical and contemporary concerns of the feminist movement
- To explore the current economic picture of women
- To understand issues and sources of discrimination and sexual harassment geared toward women
- To understand and explain the concept of the feminization of poverty
- To understand and evaluate the experience of women in education and how it is similar to their experience in the labor force
- To understand and evaluate the present situation of family life for women, including the areas of child care and housework and abortion
- To explore the political activity of women
- To learn about and evaluate the matrix of domination applied to minority women

CHAPTER OUTLINE
I.   Gender Roles
- Women are an oppressed group even though they form the numerical majority. Women in society illustrate the five characteristics of a subordinate or minority group as identified in Chapter 1.
- Biological differences have contributed to sexism. *Sexism* is the ideology that one sex is superior to the other. Quite different is the view that there are few differences between the sexes. Such an idea is expressed in the concept of *androgyny*.
- *Gender roles* are society's expectations of the proper behavior, attitudes, and activities of males and females.
- Without question, socialization has a powerful impact on the development of females and males in the United States. It may be obvious that males and females are conditioned to assume certain roles but the origin of gender roles as we know them is less clear.
- Women's role varies across different cultures. Furthermore, we know that acceptable behavior for men and women changes over time in a society.

147

II.   Sociological Perspective
- Sociologist Estelle Disch points out that gender differences are maintained in our culture through the systematic socialization of babies and infants, children, adolescents, and adults. We are bombarded with expectations for behavior as men and women from many sources simultaneously.
- Functionalists maintain the sex differentiation has contributed to overall social stability.
- Conflict theorists do not deny the presence of a differentiation by sex. In fact, they contend that the relationship between females and males has been one of unequal power, with men being dominant over women.

III.   The Feminist Movement
- Women's struggle for equality, like the struggles of other subordinate groups, has been long and multifaceted.
- In a formal sense, the American feminist movement was born in upstate New York in a town called Seneca Falls in the summer of 1848.
   A.   The Suffrage Movement
   - The *suffragists* worked for years to get women the right to vote. The opposition to giving women the right to vote came from all directions.
   - The nineteenth Amendment did not automatically lead to other feminist reforms. Women did not vote in a bloc and have not been elected to office in proportion to their numbers.
   B.   The Women's Liberation Movement
   - Ideologically, the women's movement of the 1960s had it roots in the continuing informal feminist movement that began with the first subordination of women in Western society.
   - Sociologically, several events delayed progress in the mid-1960s. The Civil Rights movement and the antiwar movement were slow to embrace women's rights.
   - The women's movement has also brought about a reexamination of men's roles.
   - Betty Freidan, a founder of the National Organization for Women (NOW), argued in the early 1960s that women had to understand the *feminine mystique*, recognizing that society saw them only as their children's mother and their husband's wife.
   C.   Listen to Our Voices: Time for Change

IV.   The Economic Picture
- Women's lower status is visible in almost all aspects of life in the United States.
- Women, more than any other group, are confined to certain occupations. Bureau of Labor Statistics researchers have compiled a "segregation index" to estimate the percentage of women who would have to change their jobs to make the distribution of men and women in each occupation mirror the relative percentage of each sex in the adult working population. The current figure is fifty-four percent.

- Although occupational segregation by gender continues, women have increased their participation in the labor force. In 1870, less than 15 percent of all workers were women, compared to 46 percent in 2004.
- A primary goal of many feminists is to eliminate sex discrimination in the labor force and the equalize job opportunities for women.

A. Sources of Discrimination
- Just as African Americans can suffer from both individual acts of racism and institutional discrimination, women are vulnerable to both sexism and institutional discrimination.
- Many efforts have been made to eliminate institutional discrimination as it applies to women. The 1964 Civil Rights Act and its enforcement arm, the Equal Employment Opportunity Commission, address cases of sex discrimination.
- *Pay equity* calls for equal pay for different types of work that are judged to be comparable by measuring such factors as employee knowledge, skills, effort, responsibility, and working conditions.
- The phrase *glass ceiling* refers to the invisible barrier blocking the promotion of a qualified worker because of gender or minority membership.
- Women are still viewed differently in the world of management. Assumptions are made that women are on a *mommy track*, an unofficial career track that firms use for women who want to divide their attention between work and family.

B. Sexual Harassment
- Under evolving legal standards, *sexual harassment* is recognized as any unwanted and unwelcome sexual advances that interfere with a person's ability to perform a job and enjoy the benefits of a job.
- Sexual harassment must be understood in the context of continuing prejudice and discrimination against women.

C. Feminization of Poverty
- Since World War II, an increasing proportion of the poor in the United States have been female, many of them divorced or never-married mothers. This alarming trend has come to be known as the *feminization of poverty*.
- According to a study based on census data, families headed by single mothers and displaced homemakers are four times more likely to live in poverty as other households in the United States. *Displaced homemakers* are defined as women whose primary occupation had been homemaking but who did not find full-time employment after being divorced, separated, or widowed.

V. Education
- The experience of women in education has been similar to their experience in the labor force: a long history of contribution, but in traditionally defined roles.
- Today, research confirms that boys and girls are treated differently in school: teachers give boys more attention. Besides receiving less attention, girls are

more likely to be encouraged to take courses that will lead them to enter lowering-paying fields of employment.

- At all levels of schooling, significant changes occurred with congressional amendments to the Education Act of 1972 and the Department of Health, Education, and Welfare guidelines developed in 1974 and 1975. Collectively called Title IX provisions, the regulations are designed to eliminate sexist practices from almost all school systems.
- Title IX is one of the most controversial steps ever taken by the federal government to promote and insure equality.

VI. Family Life

- Our society generally equates work with wages and holds unpaid work in low esteem. Women who do such work through household chores and volunteer work are given little status in our society.

   A.   Child Care and Housework

- Women are much more preoccupied than men with both thought and action with childcare and housework, but it does not end there.
- Sociologist Arlie Hochschild has used the term *second shift* to describe the double burden—work outside the home followed by child-care and housework—that many women face and that few men share equally.
- There is an economic cost to this second shift. Households do benefit from the free labor of women, but women pay what has been called the *mommy tax*: the lower salaries women receive over their lifetime because they have children

   B.   Research Focus: Housework and the Gender Divide

   C.   Abortion

- On January 22, 1973, the feminist movement received unexpected assistance from the United States Supreme Court decision in *Roe v. Wade*.
- In 1976, Congress passed the Hyde Amendment, which banned the use of Medicaid and other federal funds for abortions.
- Although courts restrict abortion, and sporadic violence near clinics continues, public opinion has remained remarkably stable over the last twenty-five years.

VII. Political Activity

- Women in the United States constitute fifty-three percent of the voting population and forty-nine percent of the labor force but only eight percent of those holding high government positions.
- In 2007, Congress included only 71 women (out of 435 members) in the House of Representatives and only 16 women (out of 100 members) in the Senate.
- Women have worked actively in both political parties, but women office holders are more likely to be Democrats by a slight margin.

VIII.   Matrix of Domination: Minority Women
- Many women experience differential treatment not only because of their gender but also because of their race and ethnicity. These citizens face a *matrix of domination*: a cumulative impact of oppression because of race, gender, and class as well as sexual orientation, religion, disability status, and age.

KEY TERMS

androgyny (p. 403)	mommy tax (p. 419)
displaced homemakers (p. 414)	mommy track (p. 413)
matrix of domination (p. 421)	pay equity (p. 411)
feminine mystique (p. 407)	second shift (p. 419)
feminization of poverty (p. 414)	sexism (p. 402)
gender roles (p. 403)	sexual harassment (p. 413)
glass ceiling (p. 413)	suffragists (p. 406)

PRACTICE TESTS

Practice Test One

True-False
1. T F *Sexism* is the ideology that one sex is superior to the other.
2. T F *Gender roles* are society's expectations of the behavior, attitudes, and activities of males and females.
3. T F Women with professional degrees earn more than their male counterparts.
4. T F According to the Department of Labor, almost three-quarters of adults who are caring for their aging parents are men.
5. T F The Supreme Court upheld the constitutionality of a 36-foor buffer zone that keeps antiabortion protestors away from a clinic entrance and parking lot.

Multiple Choice
1. The most common analogy about minorities used in the social sciences is the similarity between the status of _____ and women.
    A. men
    B. African Americans
    C. Latinos
    D. Asians

2.   Society's expectations of the proper behavior, attitudes, and activities of males and females refers to
A. androgyny.
B. sexuality.
C. gender roles.
D. sexual identity.

3.   *Functionalists* maintain that sex differentiation has contributed to overall social
_____.
A. stability
B. instability
C. change
D. imbalance

4.   The founder of the National Organization of Women is
A. Helen Gurley Brown.
B. Gloria Steinem.
C. Margaret Mead.
D. Betty Freidan.

5.   In 2004, what percentage of all workers in the United States labor force were women.
A. 38
B. 42
C. 46
D. 53

6.   Women represent _____ percent of *school teachers*.
A. 50
B. 65
C. 73
D. 90

7.   _____ calls for equal pay for different types of work that are judged to be comparable.
A. Title IX
B. Androgyny
C. Balanced pay
D. Pay equity

8.   In 2005, 12.6 percent of all families in the United States lived in *poverty*. What percentage of female headed families are living in poverty?
A. 11
B. 19
C. 28.7
D. 58

9.   What percentage of women who have children under the age of three are in the *paid labor force*?
    A. 26
    B. 38
    C. 49
    D. 57

10.   In 2007, how many women were in the United States Senate?
    A. 3
    B. 8
    C. 16
    D. 25

Short-Answer Questions

1.   What are four ways in which women represent a *minority or subordinate group*?
2.   Distinguish between *functionalist* and *conflict* views of sex differentiation in society.
3.   Briefly summarize the effects of increasing educational attainment for men and women's earnings.
4.   What are the changes that Title IX brought about in education?
5.   What is the meaning of the term *displaced homemaker*?

Practice Test Two

True-False

1.   T F   Removing barriers to equal opportunity would eventually eliminate institutional discrimination.
2.   T F   The 1964 Civil Rights Act did not apply to sex.
3.   T F   Women with doctorates earn more than their male counterparts.
4.   T F   The *mommy tax* refers to the lower salaries women receive over their lifetime because they have children.
5.   T F   Women in the U.S. constitute 53 percent of the voting population.

Multiple Choice

1.   The *feminist movement* was born in
    A. Northern California in 1875.
    B. Upstate New York in 1848.
    C. Philadelphia in 1776.
    D. Boston in 1921.

2.   Which amendment gave women the right to vote?
    A. fifteenth
    B. sixteenth
    C. nineteenth
    D. twenty-fifth

3. What percentage of accountants in the United States are women?
   A. 60
   B. 25
   C. 14
   D. 36

4. An unofficial career track that firms use for women who want to divide their attention between work and family is known as the _____.
   A. gender path
   B. ladies' tee
   C. glass ramp
   D. mommy track

5. _____ is defined as women whose primary occupation had been homemaking but who did not find full-time employment after being divorced, separated, or widowed.
   A. The feminine mystique
   B. Displaced homemakers
   C. The second shift
   D. Dual laborers

6. According to sociologist Lewis Coser and Rose Laub Coser, for women, the family is a _____ institution.
   A. weedy
   B. needy
   C. greedy
   D. seedy

7. The United States Supreme Court's decision in *Roe v. Wade* (legalizing abortion) took place in January of
   A. 1963.
   B. 1973.
   C. 1983.
   D. 1993.

8. In 1976, Congress passed the _____ which banned the use of Medicaid and other federal funds for abortions.
   A. Orson Amendment
   B. Pratt Amendment
   C. Hyde Amendment
   D. Doe Amendment

9.   Women in the United States constitute _____ percent of the *labor force*.
   A. 40
   B. 49
   C. 53
   D. 61

10.   Women have worked actively in both political parties, but women office holders are more likely to be _____ by a _____ margin.
   A. Democrats/slight
   B. Democrats/significant
   C. Republican/slight
   D. Republican/significant

Short-Answer Questions
1.   What is the evidence that our society is becoming more *androgynous*?
2.   What is meant by the *feminine mystique*?
3.   What is the evidence of the *second shift phenomenon* being experienced by women in our society?
4.   How has public opinion about *abortion* changed in our society over the last twenty-five years?
5.   What is meant by the concept *pay equity*? What are the implications of pay equity as a social policy in society?

ANSWERS TO PRACTICE TEST QUESTIONS

Practice Test One

True-False			Multiple Choice			
1.	T	(p. 403)	1.	B (p. 402)	6.	C (p. 409)
2.	T	(p. 403)	2.	C (p. 403)	7.	D (p. 411)
3.	F	(p. 412)	3.	A (p. 404)	8.	C (p. 414)
4.	F	(p. 417)	4.	D (p. 407)	9.	D (p. 419)
5.	T	(p. 420)	5.	C (p. 409)	10.	C (p. 420)

Practice Test Two

True-False			Multiple Choice			
1.	T	(p. 410)	1.	B (p. 405)	6.	C (p. 416)
2.	F	(p. 414)	2.	C (p. 406)	7.	B (p. 420)
3.	F	(p. 412)	3.	A (p. 409)	8.	C (p. 420)
4.	T	(p. 419)	4.	D (p. 413)	9.	C (p. 420)
5.	T	(p. 420)	5.	B (p. 414)	10.	A (p. 421)

APPLICATIONS/EXERCISES/ACTIVITES

1.   Analyze the Suffrage Movement from both a functionalist and a conflict
        perspective by using the material that is located at the following web site:
        http://www.rochester.edu/SBA/suffragehistory.html

2.   Changing social values have their impact on the seemingly routine daily patterns.
        This is something we should expect because interactionists argue that everyday
        behavior is dependent on the social order and its values and norms. You can read
        about this further in the article, "The Changing Door Ceremony: Notes on the
        Operations of Sex Roles in Everyday Life." in *Urban Life and Culture*, 2: 505-
        515. It is written by Laurel Richardson Walum.

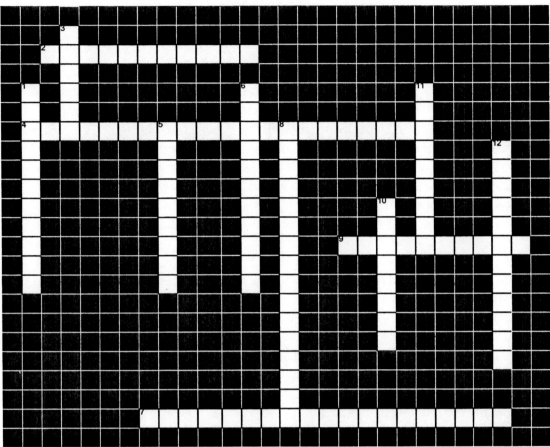

Across:

2 The double-burden ---work outside the home followed by child care and housework--that is faced by many women and that few men share equitably

4 The trend since 1970 that has women accounting for a growing proportion of those below the poverty line

7 Women whose primary occupation had been homemaking but who did not find fulltime employment after being divorced, separated, or widowed

9 an unofficial corporate career track for women who want to divide their attention between work and family

Down:

1 Women and men who worked successfully to gain women the right to vote

3 The ideology that one sex is superior to the other

5 The state of being both masculine and feminine, aggressive and gentle

6 Expectations regarding the proper behavior, attitudes, and activities of males and females

8 Society's view of a woman as only her children's mother and her husband's wife

10 Lower salaries women receive over their lifetime because they have children

11 The same wages for different types of work that are judged to be comparable by such measures as employee knowledge, skills, effort, responsibility, and working conditions; also called comparable worth

12 The barrier that blocks the promotion of a qualified worker because of gender or minority membership

Chapter Sixteen

Beyond the United States: The Comparative Perspective

CHAPTER OBJECTIVES
- To understand that subordinating people because of race, nationality, or religion is not a phenomenon unique to the United States; it occurs throughout the world
- To learn about world systems theory and ethnonational conflicts
- To gain an understanding of how racial and ethnic differences differ from society to society, focusing on Mexico, Canada, Brazil, Israel, and the Republic of South Africa
- To understand the status of women on a global level and how the global level compares to the status of women in the U.S.
- To examine the social construction of race through the application of the color gradient
- To increase an understanding of how issues of identity and culture both unify and divide communities and nations using Mexico, Canada, Brazil, Israel, and the Republic of South Africa
- To examine the foundations of the conflict between Israelis and Palestinians as well as consider the likelihood of resolution to this conflict
- To gain an understanding of the impact of colonialism and apartheid on current race relations in the Republic of South Africa
- To explore the global nature of dominant-subordinate relations along dimensions of race, ethnicity, religion, and gender

CHAPTER OUTLINE
I.   Highlights
- Confrontations between racial and ethnic groups have escalated in frequency and intensity in the twentieth century. In surveying these conflicts, we can see two themes emerge: world systems theory and ethnonational conflict. *World systems theory* considers the global economic system as divided between nations that control wealth and those that provide natural resources and labor. *Ethnonational conflict* refers to conflicts between ethnic, racial, religious, and linguistic groups within nations, which are increasingly replacing conflicts between nations as the source of refugees and even death.
- The sociological perspective concerning relations between dominant and subordinate groups treats race and ethnicity as social categories.

II.   Mexico
- In the 1520s, Spain overthrew the Aztec Indian tribe that ruled Mexico. Mexico remained a Spanish colony until the 1820s. In 1836, Texas declared its independence from Mexico and in 1846 Mexico was at war with the United States.
    - A.   The Mexican Indian People and the Color Gradient
        - In contemporary Mexico a major need has been to reassess the

relations between the indigenous peoples—the Mexican Indians, many descended from the Mayas—and the government of Mexico.

- In 2003, the Law on Indian Right and Culture went into effect.
- A *color gradient* is the placement of people on a continuum from light to dark skin color rather than in distinct racial groupings by skin color.
- In 1992, an amendment to the Mexican Constitution recognized for the first time the diverse nature of the nation.
- More than 90 percent of the indigenous populations live in houses without access to sewers, compared with 21 percent of the population as a whole.

B. The Status of Women
- Gender stratification is an example of an issue we share with almost all other countries, and Mexico is no exception. In 1975, Mexico City was the site of the first United Nations conference on the status of women.
- A 2005 survey found that eight out of ten Mexicans felt it was important to eliminate discrimination as poverty, yet 40 percent said that they did not want to live next to an Indian community and one-third considered it "normal" for women not to earn as much as men

III. Canada
- Multiculturalism is a fairly recent term in the United States; it is used to refer to diversity. In Canada, it has been adopted as a state policy for more than two decades.

A. The First Nation
- Canada, like the United States, has had an adversarial relationship with its native peoples. However, the Canadian experience has not been as violent.
- The 1.4 million native peoples of Canada are collectively referred to by the government as the First Nation or Aboriginal Peoples and represent about 3 to 6 percent of the population, depending on the definition used. This population is classified into four groups: Status Indians, Inuit, Métis, and Non-Status.
- Some of the contemporary issues facing the First Nation of Canada are very similar to those faced by Native Americans ion the United States.
- In a positive step, in 1999 Canada created a new territory in response to a native land claims in which the resident Inuit dominated Nunavut, as the territory was called, recognizes the territorial rights of the Inuit.

B. The Québécois
- Assimilation and domination have been the plight of most minority groups. The French-speaking people of the province of Quebec—the Québécois, as they are known—represent a contrasting case. Since the mid-1960s, they have reasserted their identity and captured the attention of the entire nation.
- The Québécois have sought to put French Canadian culture on an equal footing with English Canadian culture in the country as a whole and to dominate the province.

159

- Canada is characterized by the presence of two linguistic communities: the Anglophone and the Francophone.
    C. Immigration and Race
- Immigration has been a significant social force contributing to Canadian multiculturalism.
- Before 1966 Canada's immigration policy alternated between restrictive and more open, as necessary to assist the economy.
- A 2002 survey found that 54 percent of Canadians felt immigration should be reduced, and only 26 percent favored increase.

IV. Brazil: Not a Racial Paradise
    A. Legacy of Slavery
- Brazil depended much more than the United States on the slave trade. Estimates place the total number of slaved imported to Brazil at 4 million, eight times the number brought to the United States
- It is easier to recognize the continuity of African cultures among Brazil's Blacks than among Black Americans
- The most significant difference between slavery in the southern United States and in Brazil was the amount of *manumission*, the freeing of slaves.
- In Brazil, races was not seen as a measure of innate inferiority, as it was in the United States.
    B. The "Racial Democracy" Illusion
- Historically the term race is rare in Brazil. Historian Degler identified the *mulatto escape hatch* as the key to the differences in Brazilian and American race relations. It is the notion that Brazilians of mixed ancestry can move into high status positions.
- Today, the use of dozens of terms to describe oneself along the color gradient is obvious in Brazil.
- The presence of mulattoes does not mean that color is irrelevant in society or that miscegenation occurs randomly.
- In Brazil, today as in the past, light skin color enhances status, but the impact is often exaggerated.
    C. Brazilian Dilemma
- Gradually in Brazil there has been the recognition that racial prejudice and discrimination do exist.
- During the twentieth century, Brazil changed from a nation that prided itself on freedom from racial intolerance to a country legally attacking discrimination against people of color.
- Today the income disparity is significant in Brazil.
- As in other multiracial societies, women of color fare particularly poorly in Brazil. White men, of course, have the highest income, whereas Black men have earning levels comparable to those of White women, and Afro-Brazilian women are the furthest behind.
- The challenge to Afro-Brazilians becoming more organized is not that

they fail to recognize the discrimination but that the society tends to think that the distinctions are based on social class.

V.   Israel and the Palestinians
- Nearly 2,000 years ago, the Jews were exiled from Palestine in the *Diaspora*. The exiled Jews settled throughout Europe and elsewhere in the Middle East.

   A.   Arab-Israeli Conflicts
   - No sooner had Israel been recognized than the Arab nations announced their intention to restore control of the Palestinian Arabs, by force if necessary.
   - In 1967, Egypt, followed by Syria, responded to Israel's military actions to take surrounding territory in what has come to be called the Six-Day War. The October 1973 war (called the Yom Kippur War by the Jews and the Ramadan War by Arabs), launched against Israel by Egypt and Syria.
   - The secular Jews feel pressure from the more traditional and ultra-Orthodox Jews, who push for a nation more reflective of Jewish customs and laws.

   B.   The Intifada
   - The *Intifada*, the uprising against Israel by the Palestinians in the occupied territories through attacks against soldiers, the boycott of Israeli goods, general strikes, resistance, and no cooperation with Israeli authorities.
   - Nearly half of the world's Palestinian people live under Israeli control.
   - The Intifada and international reaction propelled Israel and the PLO to reach an agreement in 1993 known as the Oslo Accords.

   C.   The Search for Solutions Amid Violence
   - Politically, the creation of a Palestinian Authority had been an unexpected achievement, but economically, the people actually are worse off.
   - Hard-liners on both sides grew resistant to the move toward separate recognized Palestinian and Israel states.
   - The immediate problem is to end the violence, but any lasting peace must face a series of difficult issues, including the status of Jerusalem, the future of the Jewish settlements in the Palestinian territories, the future of Palestinians and other Arabs with Israeli citizenship, the creation of a truly independent Palestinian national state, and the future of Palestinian refugees elsewhere.

VI.   Republic of South Africa
   A.   The Legacy of Colonialism
   - The permanent settlement of South Africa by Europeans began in 1652, when the Dutch East India Company established a colony in Cape Town as a port of call for shipping vessels bound for India. The Boers, seminomads descended from the Dutch, did not remain on the coast but trekked inland to establish vast sheep and cattle ranches.

161

- *Pass laws* were introduced, placing curfews on the Bantus and limiting their geographic movement.
B. Listen To Our Voices: Africa, It Is Ours!
C. Apartheid
- In 1948, South Africa was granted its independence from the United Kingdom, and the National Party, dominated by Afrikaners, assumed control of the government.
- *Apartheid* came to mean a policy of separate development. Apartheid can perhaps be best understood as a twentieth-century effort to reestablish the master-slave relationship.
D. The Era of Reconciliation and Moving On
- In April 1994, South Africa held its first universal election. Apartheid was ended.
- A significant step to help South Africa move past apartheid was the creation of Truth and Reconciliation Commission (TRC).
- Some of the controversial issues facing the African National Council (ANC)-led government are: desperate poverty, affirmative action, medical care, crime, and school integration.
- The government has pledged to address the issue of land ownership.
- Under the 1994 Restitution of Land Rights Act, the displaced citizens can now file for a return of their land.
E. Research Focus: Listening to the People

KEY TERMS

apartheid (p. 446)

color gradient (p. 429)

Diaspora (p. 440)

ethnonational conflict (p. 426)

quilombo (p. 437)

mulatto escape hatch (p. 437)

Intifada (p. 442)

pass laws (p. 446)

world systems theory (p. 426)

Zionism (p. 440)

visible minorities (p. 417)

PRACTICE TESTS

Practice Test One

True-False
1.   T F   Women in Mexico receive the right to vote in 1910.
2.   T F   The Canadian experience with native peoples has historically been more violent than the relations between native people and the United States government.
3.   T F   Canada never had a system of slavery.
4.   T F   Nearly half of the world's Palestinian people live under Israeli control.
5.   T F   The Boers is a group of seminomads descended from the Dutch and living in South Africa.

Multiple Choice
1.   The status of Indians in Canada is considered an example of
      A. segregation.
      B. pluralism.
      C. assimilation.
      D. fusion.

2.   The Dominion of Canada formed independent of England in
      A. 1857.
      B. 1899.
      C. 1909.
      D. 1940.

3.   As of 2004, women accounted for _____ percent of Mexico's National Assembly.
      A. 12
      B. 17
      C. 23
      D. 29

4.   The existence of at least _____ Indian cultures has been seen in this century in Mexico.
      A. 36
      B. 46
      C. 56
      D. 66

5.   In 1994, rebels from an armed insurgent group called the _____ National Liberation Army seized 4 towns in the state of Chiapas in southern Mexico.
      A. Bautista
      B. Patatista
      C. Zapatista
      D. Mapatista

6.   The population of native Canadians living in the northern part of the country, who typically have been called the Eskimos are known as
A. Status Indians.
B. Non-Status Indians.
C. Métis.
D. Inuit.

7.   Slavery officially continued in Canada until
A. 1833.
B 1890.
C. Canada never had a system of slavery.
D. 1902.

8.   Nearly 2000 years ago, the Jews were exiled from Palestine in the _____.
A. Ramadan War
B. Intifada
C. Zionist War
D. Diaspora

9.   Egypt recognized Israel's existence in
A. 1948.
B. 1959.
C. 1979.
D. Egypt has never recognized the existence of Israel.

10.   In South Africa, seminomads descended from the Dutch who trekked inland to establish vast sheep farms are known as the
A. Coloureds.
B. Boers.
C. Osloewns.
D. Bantus.

Short-Answer Questions
1.   What factors in the last couple of decades have been involved in the resumption of interethnic conflict?
2.   What are the goals of the Zapatista National Liberation Army?
3.   Who are the Québécois?
4.   What was *apartheid*?
5.   What was the *Diaspora*?

Practice Test Two

True-False
1.   T F   In 1900, the majority of the Mexican population still spoke the Indian language.
2.   T F   Immigration has been a significant social force contributing to Canadian multiculturalism.
3.   T F   Quilombos are hideaways.
4.   T F   *Diaspora* is a term referring to the return of the Jews to Palestine.
5.   T F   *Apartheid* in South Africa ended in 1971.

Multiple Choice
1. _____ conflict refers to conflicts between ethnic, racial, religious, and linguistic groups within a nation.
   A. Endosocietal
   B. Ethnonational
   C. Exonational
   D. Intraethnic

2. At the top of the color gradient in Mexico are the
   A. mestizos.
   B. mesas.
   C. criollos.
   D. texocas.

3. Among the Aboriginal peoples of Canada. People of mixed ancestry are classified as
   A. Non-Status.
   B. Status.
   C. Métis.
   D. Inuit.

4. The Québécois are the
   A. French-speaking people of Quebec.
   B. elected officials from Quebec.
   C. Native peoples of Canada.
   D. Black Canadians.

5. ____ depended much more than the United States on the slave trade.
   A. Brazil
   B. Mexico
   C. The Republic of South Africa
   D. Israel

6.	Brazil uses a _____ to define race.
	A. mestizo
	B. quilombo
	C. manumission
	D. color gradient

7.	The Six Day War occurred in
	A. 2130 B.C.E.
	B. 70 A.D.
	C. 1948.
	D. 1967.

8.	Which of the following locations is farthest north?
	A. the Gaza Strip
	B. the West Bank
	C. the Golan Heights
	D. the Dead Sea

9.	In 2005, what percentage of the South African population was White?
	A. 2
	B. 9.4
	C. 20
	D. 30

10.	Black tribal groups in South Africa are collectively called
	A. Inuit.
	B. Bantus.
	C. Mbuti.
	D. Kung

Short-Answer Questions
1.	Briefly describe the history of slavery in Brazil.
2.	What is the *Intifada*?
3.	What are four of the controversial issues facing the ANC-led government in South Africa?
4.	What were *pass laws?*
5.	What is *Zionism*?

ANSWERS TO PRACTICE TEST QUESTIONS

Practice Test One

True-False		Multiple Choice			
1.	F (p. 430)	1.	B (p. 428)	6.	D (p. 432)
2.	F (p. 432)	2.	A (p. 428)	7.	A (p. 435)
3.	F (p. 435)	3.	C (p. 412)	8.	D (p. 440)
4.	T (p. 443)	4.	C (p. 429)	9.	C (p. 441)
5.	T (p. 445)	5.	C (p. 411)	10.	B (p. 445)

Practice Test Two

True-False		Multiple Choice			
1.	T (p. 429)	1.	B (p. 426)	6.	D (p. 437)
2.	T (p. 435)	2.	C (p. 429)	7.	D (p. 441)
3.	T (p. 437)	3.	C (p. 432)	8.	C (p. 442)
4.	F (p. 440)	4.	A (p. 433)	9.	B (p. 445)
5.	F (p. 446)	5.	A (p. 437)	10.	B (p. 446)

APPLICATIONS/EXERCISES/ACTIVITIES

1. Use the conflict, labeling and functionalist approaches to assess the current situation in Northern Ireland using the material that you find at the following web site as the basis for your discussion: http://headlines.yahoo.com/Full_Coverage/World/Northern_Ireland_Conflict/

2. Discuss how residents of the strife-torn country of Northern Ireland use people's first names to determine whether or not they are Roman Catholics or Protestants. Locate the article, "Telling It Like It Is, " in *New Society*, 65: 288. Do you think this is a valid way to determine what religion someone is?

Chapter 16 – Beyond the United States: The Comparative Perspective

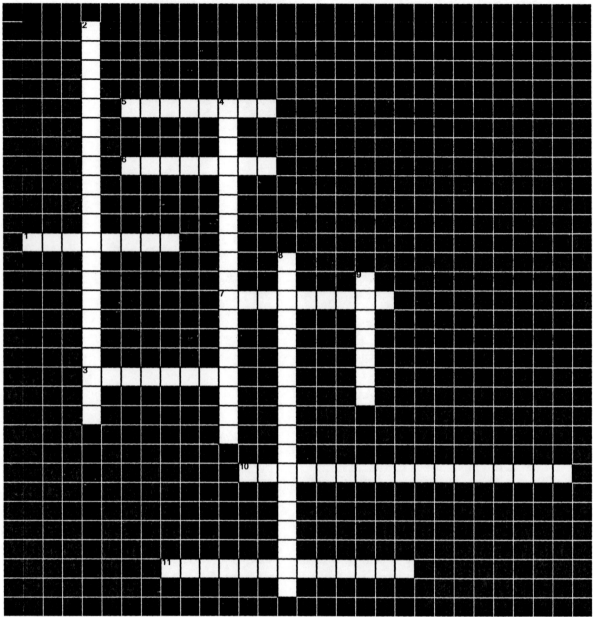

Across:

1   The exile of Jews from Palestine
3   The Palestinian uprising against Israeli authorities in the occupied territories
5   Slave hideaways in Brazil
6   Laws that controlled internal movement by non-Whites in South Africa
7   The policy of the South African government intended to maintain separation of Blacks, Coloureds, and Asians from the dominant Whites
10   In Canada, persons other than Aboriginal or First Nation people who are non-white in racial background
11   The placement of people on a continuum from light to dark skin rather than in distinct racial groupings by skin color

Down:

2   Conflicts between ethnic, racial, religious, and linguistic groups within nations replacing conflicts between nations
4   Notion that Brazilians of mixed ancestry can move into high status positions
8   A view of the global economic system as divided between nations that control wealth and those that provide natural resources and labor
9   Traditional Jewish religious yearning to return to the biblical homeland, now used to refer to support for the state of Israel

Chapter Seventeen

Overcoming Exclusion

CHAPTER OBJECTIVES
- To understand that the experience of social disadvantage if not limited to groups defined by race, ethnicity, gender, or religion
- To understand how the elderly are still a group at a disadvantage, given the ageism in our society
- To understand how and why older people in the United States are subject to a paradox
- To explore the advocacy efforts by the elderly
- To understand the process and consequences of labeling the disabled
- To explore the ways in which people with disabilities have sought to achieve both respect and opportunities
- To understand how the Americans with Disabilities Act (ADA) is a significant step forward
- To explore the advocacy efforts by the disabled
- To understand and evaluate how long-term homophobia has made it a challenge for gays and lesbians to go about their lives
- To explore the advocacy efforts for gay and lesbian rights
- To understand even though there has been progress made for each of these groups, as well as the racial and ethnic minorities discussed earlier, there still remains a full agenda for further progress

CHAPTER OUTLINE
I. The Aged: A Social Minority
- Older people in the United States are subject to a paradox. While on the one hand they have been viewed with negative stereotypes and are subject to discrimination, on the other hand they have successfully organized themselves into a potent collective force.
- The elderly share the characteristics of subordinate or minority groups that were introduced in Chapter 1.
- A. Who Are the Elderly?
  - In the twentieth century, the number of people in the United States under the age of sixty-five tripled. At the same time, the number of people over the age of sixty-five increased eleven-fold.
  - Elderly women outnumber men by a ratio of 3 to 2. About eighty-three percent of the elderly are White.
- B. Ageism
  - In 1968, physician Robert Butler, the founding director of the National Institute on Aging, coined the term *ageism* to refer to prejudice and discrimination against the elderly.
  - The federal Age Discrimination in Employment Act, which went into

effect in 1968, was passed to protect workers 40 years of age or older from being fired because of their age and replaced with younger workers who presumable would receive lower salaries.

    C.   Research Focus: The Face of Ageism

    D.   The Economic Picture

- There is significant variation in wealth and poverty among the nation's older people. As a group, older people in the United States are neither homogeneous nor poor.
- The typical elderly person enjoys a standard of living that is much higher than at any point in the nation's past.

    E.   Advocacy Efforts By the Elderly

- One group working on behalf of the elderly is the Gray Panthers.
- The growing collective consciousness among older people also contributed to the establishment of the Older Women's League (OWL) in 1980.
- The largest organization representing the nation's elderly is the American Association of Retired Persons (AARP), founded in 1958.
- Although organizations like the Gray Panthers, OWL, and AARP are valuable, the diversity of the nation's older population necessitates many different responses to problems of the elderly.

II.   People with Disabilities: Moving On

    A.   Disability In Contemporary Society

- Today, an estimated 51.2 million people had a disability in 2002. *Disability* is considered a reduced ability to perform tasks one would normally do at a given stage in life.
- Disabilities are found in all segments of the population, but racial and ethnic minorities are disproportionately more likely to experience them and also to have less access to assistance.
- Although disability knows no social class, about two-thirds of working-age people with a disability in the United States are unemployed.

    B.   Labeling the Disabled

- Labeling theorists, drawing on the work of sociologist Erving Goffman, suggest that society attaches a stigma to many forms of disability and that this stigma leads to prejudicial treatment.
- As with other subordinate statuses, the mass media have contributed to the stereotyping of people with disabilities.
- People with disabilities face challenges to being taken seriously as job applicants, and research shows that the problems intensify further for members of racial and ethnic minorities with disabilities.
- Society is sometimes organized in a way that limits people with disabilities through institutional discrimination.

    C.   Listen To Our Voices: The Magic Wand

    D.   Advocacy for the Disability Rights

- Since World War II, there has been a steadily growing effort to ensure not only the survival of people with disabilities but also the same rights as enjoyed by others.

- Disability rights activists argue that there is an important distinction between organizations *for* disabled people and organizations *of* disabled people.
- Many organizations worked for the 1990 passage of the Americans with Disabilities Act (ADA). The ADA has generated public discussion on how to address the artificial limitations confronting people with disabilities.
- *Visitability* refers to making private homes built to be accessible for visitors with disabilities.
- Activists remain encouraged since the passage of the ADA.

III. Gays and Lesbians: Coming Out for Equality
   A. Being Gay and Lesbian in the United States
   - In the 1920s and 1930s, homosexuality became visible in the U.S.
   - It is hard to get accurate data on gays and lesbians.
   - In 2004, in Rhea County, Tennessee, a measure was passed that allowed the county to prosecute someone for being gay or lesbian as a "crime against nature."
   B. Prejudice and Discrimination
   - *Homophobia*, the fear of and prejudice toward homosexuality, is present in every facet of life: the family, organized religion, the workplace, official policies, and the mass media.
   - In 2005, fifty-six percent of the public felt that homosexual relations should not be legal. In some cases, antigay prejudice has led to violence.
   - In 1998 Matthew Shepherd's brutal murder shocked the nation.
   C. Advocacy for Gay and Lesbian Rights
   - The first homosexual organization in the United States was founded in Chicago in 1924.
   - The contemporary gay and lesbian movement marks its beginning in New York City on June 28, 1969.
   - Despite the efforts of the gay and lesbian rights movement there have been a number of significant Supreme Court decisions that have been unfavorable to the rights of homosexuals.
   - Many states recognize *domestic partnerships*, defined as two unrelated adult who have chosen to share one another's lives in a relationship of mutual caring, who reside together and agree to be jointly responsible for their dependents, basic living expenses, and other common necessities.
   - A 2006 survey showed that only thirty-nine percent felt that same-sex marriages should be legal.

IV.   The Glass Half Empty
- For many people, the progress of subordinate groups or minorities—the half-full glass—makes it difficult to understand calls for more programs and new reforms.
- In absolute terms, the glass of water has been filling up, but people in the early twenty-first century do not compare themselves with people in the 1960s.
- The nation's largest minority groups, African Americans and Hispanics, have higher household income, complete more schooling, and enjoy longer life expectancy today than in 1975. White Americans have made similar strides in all three areas. The gap remains and, if one analyzes it closely, has actually increased in some instances.
- As the United States promotes racial, ethnic, and religious diversity, it strives also to impose universal criteria on employers, educators, and realtors so that subordinate racial and ethnic groups can participate fully in the larger society.
- Relations between racial, ethnic, or religious groups take two broad forms, as situations characterized by either consensus or conflict.

KEY TERMS

ageism (p. 456)   homophobia (p. 468)

disability (p. 461)   visitability (p. 466)

domestic partnership (p. 470)

PRACTICE TESTS

Practice Test One

True-False
1.   T F   Elderly women outnumber elderly men by a ratio of 3 to 2 in the United States.
2.   T F   Poverty rates for elderly women in the United States are higher today across racial and ethnic groups than they were twenty years ago.
3.   T F   Over fifty percent of the adults in the United States believe homosexuality should be *illegal*.
4.   T F   Homophobia is the fear and prejudice toward homosexuals.
5.   T F   Most White adults in the United States over the age of twenty-five have a *college degree*.

Multiple Choice

1. The image of the melting pot is not invoked as much today. Instead people speak of a _____ to describe a country that is ethnically diverse.
   A. bowl of fruit
   B. fruit cake
   C. apple pie
   D. salad bowl

2. About _____ percent of the elderly are white.
   A. 90
   B. 80
   C. 70
   D. 60

3. Among elderly Whites, the poverty rate in 2000 was _____ percent.
   A. 2
   B. 8
   C. 13
   D. 21

4. Today, an estimated one in _____ people in the United States has a disability.
   A. 24
   B. 18
   C. 9
   D. 6

5. _____ refers to making private home built to be accessible for visitors with disabilities.
   A. Displacement
   B. Advocacy
   C. Visitability
   D. Desirability

6. The fear of and prejudice toward homosexuality is known as
   A. gayphobia.
   B. queerphilia.
   C. homophobia.
   D. penilephobia.

7. The most outspoken AIDS activist group as been
   A. OWL.
   B. ADA.
   C. ACT-UP.
   D. BE-ME.

8.	Several states now recognize _____, defined as two unrelated adults of the same sex who have chosen to share one another's lives in a relationship of mutual caring, who reside together and agree to be jointly responsible.
	A.	home bundles
	B.	cohabitants
	C.	house tracts
	D.	domestic partnerships

9.	In 2003, twenty-seven percent of Whites over the age of twenty-five had a college degree. What was the corresponding percentage for Hispanics?
	A.	5
	B.	11
	C.	17
	D.	22

10.	In 1975, thirty-one percent of Blacks were poor. What percentage of Blacks in the United States was poor in 2003?
	A.	19
	B.	24
	C.	31
	D.	42

Short-Answer Questions

1.	What is meant by the concept of the *salad bowl* in terms of describing ethnic diversity?
2.	Briefly describe the demographic picture of the elderly in the United States today.
3.	What is the *labeling* issue regarding disability as developed by Erving Goffman?
4.	Briefly describe the history in the United States of the gay and lesbian movement.
5.	What are two conclusions being made by the author concerning the issue of *overcoming exclusion*?

Practice Test Two

True-False

1.	T F	By 2050, people over the age of sixty-five are expected to represent over one-third of the population of the United States.
2.	T F	Although firing someone simply because she or he is old violates federal laws, courts have upheld the right to layoff older workers for economic reasons.
3.	T F	The elderly in the United States are better off today financially and physically than ever before.
4.	T F	The first homosexual organization in the United States was founded in New York City in 1969.
5.	T F	The *median household income* of Hispanics in 2005 was higher than that for Blacks.

Multiple Choice

1. The elderly in the United States are a
    A. growing segment of the population
    B. decreasing segment of the population
    C. statistically constant segment of the population
    D. small segment of the population

2. The federal Age Discrimination Employment Act, which went into effect in 1968, was passed to protect workers _____ years of age or older.
    A. 18
    B. 21
    C. 40
    D. 65

3. Among the following groups of elderly, which had the highest rate of poverty in 2005?
    A. Whites
    B. Blacks
    C. Hispanics
    D. Asians and Pacific Islanders

4. The largest organization representing the nation's elderly is the
    A. AARP.
    B. Gray Panthers.
    C. OWL.
    D. ACT.

5. Among ____ of working-age people with a disability in the U.S. are unemployed.
    A. one-third
    B. one-half
    C. two-thirds
    D. three-fourths

6. The group known as the *Rolling Quads* refers to an organization of
    A. Black cyclists.
    B. aged nursing home residents.
    C. women bikers over the age of sixty-five.
    D. disabled students.

7. Researchers of the National Health and Life Survey and the Voter News Service estimate that ____ percent of United States adults are gay or lesbian.
    A. 2 to 5
    B. 7 to 8
    C. 9 to 12
    D. 14 to 15

8. The contemporary gay and lesbian movement marks it beginning in
   A. Boston.
   B. San Francisco.
   C. Chicago.
   D. New York City.

9. The Defense of Marriage Act of 1996
   A. denied federal recognition of same-sex marriages.
   B. supported federal recognition of same-sex marriages.
   C. was immensely unpopular with the public.
   D. established domestic partner benefits.

10. The metaphor of the glass half empty refers to
    A. the progress made to date for subordinate groups.
    B. the progress still to be achieved for all minorities.
    C. the paradox of income and education change.
    D. civil rights for gays and lesbians.

Short-Answer Questions

1. What is the evidence for the presence of *ageism* in the United States today?
2. Briefly describe the economic status of the elderly in the United States today.
3. The Americans with Disabilities Act does not take the perspective that disability is an entitlement issue. What is meant by this statement?
4. Briefly describe the contemporary legal status of homosexuality in the United States.
5. Explain the point that the *glass is half empty* as presented in the text. Make reference to empirical evidence regarding this concept.

ANSWERS TO PRACTICE TEST QUESTIONS

Practice Test One

True-False		Multiple Choice			
1.	T (p. 456)	1.	D (p. 454)	6.	C (p. 468)
2.	F (p. 458)	2.	A (p. 456)	7.	C (p. 469)
3.	T (p. 471)	3.	B (p. 459)	8.	D (p. 470)
4.	T (p. 468)	4.	D (p. 461)	9.	B (p. 472)
5.	F (p. 472)	5.	C (p. 466)	10.	A (p. 472)

Practice Test Two

True-False	**Multiple Choice**			
1.	F (p. 455)	1.	A (p. 455)	6.	D (p. 464)
2.	T (p. 457)	2.	C (p. 457)	7.	A (p. 467)
3.	T (p. 460)	3.	B (p. 459)	8.	D (p. 469)
4.	F (p. 469)	4.	A (p. 460)	9.	A (p. 472)
5.	T (p. 472)	5.	C (p. 444)	10.	B (p. 471)

APPLICATIONS/EXERCISES/ACTIVITIES

1. The two web sites that are noted below focus on historical overviews. One site focuses on the history and accomplishments of people with disabilities, and the other site focuses on gays and lesbians. Go to these sites and use the labeling, conflict, and functionalist approaches to examine these two histories and to make comparisons and contrasts between them. The sites are:
    http://www.disabilityhistory.org/dshp.html
    and http://www.pbs.org/outofthepast/

2. Identify two couples who you can ask how they balance out their work and family life. One couple should be younger and the other one should be older. Both couples should have children. Ask them the following questions:
    *   How did becoming a parent change your relationship with each other?
    *   How did raising children affect your finances?
    *   If you were employed when your first child was born, how did becoming a parent change things? For example, did you work more hours, or change from a full-time to a part-time job?
    *   Did having children affect your education?
    *   When were you the most satisfied being a parent and why?
    *   When were you the most stressed out about being a parent and why?

    After you have interviewed both couples, individually respond to the following questions:
    *   What similarities and differences did you encounter between couples? What differences did you note?
    *   How did your subjects balance work and family? Did having children affect both couples similarly? What differences did you find?
    *   Did you come across a "mommy track" in employment patterns?
    *   Compare and contrast the couples' responses to their experiences of balancing work, family life, and parenting. Did you encounter any age or gender differences in their parenting styles?

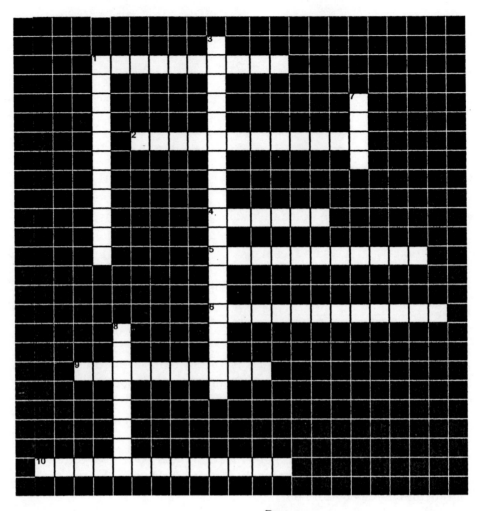

Across:
1   The fear of and prejudice toward homosexuality
2   Building private homes to be accessible for visitors with disabilities
4   Prejudice and discrimination against the elderly
5   People who see themselves as the sex opposite of their birth identity
6   This group established the Berkeley Center for Independent Living, which became the model for hundreds of independent living centers
9   A reduced ability to perform tasks one would normally do at a given stage in life
10   Cross-dressers who wear clothing of the opposite sex

Down:
1   People with same-gendered attraction
3   Two unrelated adults who have chosen to share on another's lives in a relationship of mutual caring who reside together, and who agree to be jointly responsible for their dependents, basic living expenses, and other common necessities
7   The name for male homosexuals
8   The name for female homosexuals